Biblical Faith and Fathering

Why We Call God "Father"

JOHN W. MILLER

Paulist Press/New York and New Jersey

For Larry and Karen,
Emily, Jessica, and Stephanie

Acknowledgements: Paulist Press gratefully acknowledges use of the following: "God as Father in the Bible and the Father Image in Several Contemporary Ancient Near East Myths: A Comparison," *Studies in Religion* 14/3, pp. 347–354 used with permission of Canadian Corporation for Studies in Religion; "The Contemporary Fathering Crisis: The Bible and Research Psychology," *The Conrad Grebel Review*, Fall 1983, pp. 21–37 used with permission of Conrad Grebel College, Waterloo, Ontario; "Depatriarchalizing God in Biblical Interpretation: A Critique," *The Catholic Biblical Quarterly* 48/4, pp. 609–616 used with permission.

Library of Congress Cataloging-in-Publication Data

Miller, John W., 1926–
    Biblical faith and fathering: why we call God
"Father" / John W. Miller.
        p.   cm.
    Includes bibliographical references.
    ISBN 0-8091-3107-2 : $7.95 (est.)
    1. Patriarchy—Biblical teaching.   I. Title.
BS680.P36M55   1990
231'.1—dc20   89-37716
                                                                CIP

Published by Paulist Press
997 Macarthur Boulevard
Mahwah, New Jersey 07430

Printed and bound in the
United States of America

CONTENTS

PART IV: CONTEMPORARY ISSUES

Modern society counts too easily on the domestication of man. The great upheavals of history show us that no part of his cultural adaptation is so secure that it can be relied on as a permanent human possession.*

*Alexander Mitscherlich, *Society without the Father* (New York: Harcourt, Brace and World, 1963), p. 303.

PREFACE

When I first wrote the following essays, I had no intention of ever publishing them as a collection. Several were prepared for scholarly journals; most were drafted as lectures. Someday, I thought, I will try to address this subject in a less scholarly manner. When I finally got around to doing so, however, I found myself wondering whether the scholarly mode was not more what was needed right now. The conviction had been growing that there were important omissions and distortions in the current analysis and critique of biblical patriarchy. The feeling was also growing that these can be rectified only by a careful consideration of certain rather complex theoretical and exegetical issues.

It was thoughts such as these that prompted the effort to rewrite, edit and assemble these essays in a single volume. Each essay is headed with a brief synopsis of its contents. An attempt is also made in the Introduction (Chapter 1) and Conclusion (Chapter 10) to indicate how each fits into a larger pattern and what their collective relevance might be, especially for Christians.

Four of these essays were previously published in scholarly journals.[1] I thank their editors for permission to republish them here with minor revisions. I am also grateful to the adults of the Akron Mennonite Church for their helpful feedback on the occasion of our discussion of these issues at their School of Adult Studies during the summer of 1986. Ben Meyer, Elizabeth Achtemeier, Paul Nathanson, Jack Harrison, Alex Molnar, Vernard Eller and Abraham Schmidt graciously consented to read the manuscript in its penultimate form and share their comments. Their willingness to do so was greatly appreciated, as were also the substantive editorial suggestions of Fr. Lawrence Boadt.

Our daughter Karen, her husband Larry and their three

children, Emily, Jessica, and Stephanie, were house guests during the weeks when I was preparing the final draft of this manuscript. Their presence in our home was a daily reminder of the importance of parenting. This book is gratefully dedicated to them and many young families like them who in the face of innumerable pressures to do otherwise are building a loving, caring life together.

Note

1. "In Defense of Monotheistic Father Religion," *The Journal of Religion and Health*, Spring 1983; "The Contemporary Fathering Crisis: The Bible and Research Psychology," *The Conrad Grebel Review*, Fall 1983; "God as Father in the Bible and the Father Image in Several Contemporary Ancient Near Eastern Myths: A Comparison," *Studies in Religion/Sciences Religieuses*, Summer 1985; "Depatriarchalizing God in Biblical Interpretation: A Critique," *The Catholic Biblical Quarterly*, October 1986.

INTRODUCTION

הֲל֣וֹא אָ֤ב אֶחָד֙ לְכֻלָּ֔נוּ
הֲ ל֤וֹא אֵ֤ל אֶחָד֙ בְּרָאָ֔נוּ

Have we not all one father?
Has not one God created us?*

* Malachi 2:10. Biblical citations are from the Revised Standard Version unless otherwise indicated.

PROBLEM AND OVERVIEW

Too little attention has been paid in recent critiques of biblical patriarchy to the fact that the father-involved family is a fragile cultural achievement that cannot be taken for granted. When this and other still neglected matters are taken into consideration, the precise nature of the contribution of biblical faith to a high culture of fathering can be better appreciated.

Previously taken for granted or even eulogized, the Bible's focus on fathers is now regarded by many as patriarchal and sexist. As a consequence it has come under repeated critique and attack. Indeed, some have concluded that the Bible is so hopelessly prejudiced in this regard that there is no alternative but to abandon it. Others, still believing that biblical faith might be salvaged, have set themselves the task of changing it.

Some of the more radical changes being advocated today have to do with the biblical portrait of *God* as father.[1] If God is father, some argue, then males are permitted to regard themselves as god-like in ways females cannot. This is demeaning to women, they say. Thus, if we are ever to move beyond the Bible's sexist outlook, we must degenderize this notion of God either by extinguishing it, or by replacing it with gender-neutral terms such as creator, redeemer, spirit, or by balancing it with feminine images. God is to be thought of as "she" as well as "he," as "her" as well as "him."

There are still many, however, who experience innovations such as these as unsettling. How is it possible, they ask, that biblical faith, so life-giving for so many for so long, is now suddenly to be regarded as so fundamentally flawed that a virtual rewrite of its God-language is required? Were previous generations really this mistaken? Is the biblical preoccupation with fathers and fathering really as prejudicial against women as is now often assumed?[2]

In the essays that follow I seek to address these questions by examining a number of issues that I regard as highly relevant but much neglected or overlooked in the discussions to date. The following is a brief synopsis of the topics I will be addressing.

• Many critics of biblical patriarchalism seem to assume that fathering in the psychological sense is something that can be taken for granted. The problem as they see it is in the *excess* of paternal power and prerogative that so often manifests itself there. This analysis, however, is almost invariably carried out without the benefit of any conception of what in fact is involved in the male of the species taking on a paternal role in a two-parent family. Because of this it is also often not recognized that fathering is a predominantly cultural achievement, due to the fact that it is so much less nature-determined than is mothering. This is why an inevitable drift occurs in a given society in the direction of fatherless families headed by mothers alone when it fails to support the father-*involved* family—a situation only too familiar to those of us living in North America today. Laying bare the pre-conditions for the emergence and continuance of a pattern of involvement of fathers in the care and nurture of their own children (Chapter 2) is the essential starting point for an analysis and appreciation of the contributions of biblical faith to this realm of human existence.

• Equally neglected in recent discussions is some consideration of the dynamics of *the particular form* of the father-involved family that prevailed in the ancient near east of biblical times. It has long been recognized that certain reproductive notions were important factors in this regard—the discovery of the role that semen plays in human reproduction, in particular. But without a prior understanding of the conditions necessary for father-involvement in the first place (as outlined in Chapter 2), the impact of this biological discovery on the formation of the two-parent family could not be properly assessed. Nor has it been sufficiently recognized how already at the dawn of the biblical period some of the more problematic features of ancient near eastern patriarchalism had already been identified and confronted, including the issue of a child's right-to-life, the sine qua non of a culture of fathering. These are the issues I address in my second essay (Chapter 3).

• In my third and fourth essays, the focus shifts to an analysis of the revelation of *God* as father in biblical tradition. Superficial assumptions regarding what this entailed and how this achievement relates to the Bible's cultural background are widespread. Many seem to think, for example, that the biblical portrait of God's fatherliness simply mirrors the prevailing paternal stereotypes of the ancient near east in which it arose. How wrong this is becomes evident, however, as one compares the biblical portrait of God as father with contemporary images of father-gods in the myths of that region. In doing so one quickly discovers that ancient Egyptian, Canaanite or Mesopotamian religions were by no means as patriarchal as commonly assumed. More active and powerful by far than the father-deities in these regions were son, mother and daughter deities. Seen in this light the uniqueness of the biblical revelation becomes more tangible. A look at the biblical representation of God as father within its cultural context in antiquity is the subject of my third essay (Chapter 4).

• Another misunderstanding is the now widespread belief that the Bible is not nearly as patriarchal in its representation of God as once thought. There are within the Bible itself, it is claimed, "depatriarchalizing" tendencies—texts which depict God as feminine as well as masculine, or as a deity beyond gender altogether. The evidence put forward in support of these suggestions is far from cogent, however. Not once in biblical tradition is God ever spoken of as "she" or "her" or regarded as genderless. On the other hand, God is not portrayed there simply as male either, but as a father whose tenderness and compassion are often mother-*like*. In no instance does this imply that God has become a mother-figure to his worshippers. The uniformity of the canonical representation of God as father is one of its most notable features. These are the issues I address in my fourth essay (Chapter 5).

• Israel's faith in *God* as dynamically caring father created an environment that gave birth to new modes of *human* fathering. This is the topic of my fifth and sixth essays (Chapters 6 and 7). In them I seek to show how, to an extent unparalleled in the world of antiquity, faith and fathering came to be linked in Israel through a complex of fathering rituals (such as the redemption of the first-born, circumcision and passover)—rituals carried out by fathers within the setting of their biological families. It was by this means, I suggest, that Israelite fathers came to be vested with an identity and a sense of care for their children that was religiously based and exceptional, giving birth in time to one of the most father-involved patterns of fathering on earth. This family environment was the setting within which Christianity was born, and out of which it generated its own peculiar stance toward fathering—one continuous with, and yet significantly different from, its Jewish heritage.

• In my seventh and eighth essays (Chapters 8 and 9), I seek to indicate some of the roots and reasons for our contemporary fathering crisis and how the biblical tradition of fathering may be relevant to our efforts at surmounting it. It is at this point that my essays become most explicitly apologetic. Not only, I argue, is there a remarkable congruence between the Bible and modern research psychology in their mutual attitudes toward fathering and its importance, but viewed in the light of what we now know about the psychological development of children of both sexes, one can begin to sense why the biblical revelation of God's fatherliness has in fact been such a blessing for the communities worldwide that have embraced it. As biblical law codes and covenants so confidently declare, those shall live long in the land who follow this God and his precepts.

• My final essay (Chapter 10) is an attempt at indicating the possible relevance of the prior essays by asking what in this light some of our more obvious weaknesses and strengths as North American Christians might be, so far as a recovery of stronger fathering traditions is concerned. The way ahead will not be easy,

I suggest, due in part to certain inherently ambivalent attitudes toward the father-involved family in western democratic tradition, as well as within Christianity itself. The western democratic ideals of equality and freedom are not necessarily congenial to family values, and Christianity has traditionally paid more attention to the needs of the spiritual family of the church than to developing a spiritual support system for the biological family. Nevertheless, there are specific things we might be doing, and my study concludes with a few suggestions of what some of these might be.

Notes

1. For a helpful review of the feminist critique of biblical god-language, see Carol P. Christ, "Symbols of Goddess and God in Feminist Theology," in *The Book of the Goddess Past and Present*, Carl Olson, ed. (New York: Crossroad, 1985), pp. 231–251.
2. For an incisive critical response to recent feminist proposals, see Roland M. Frye, *Language for God and Feminist Language, Problems and Principles*, Reports from the Center, Number 3 (Princeton: Center of Theological Inquiry, 50 Stockton Street, 1988); Elizabeth Achtemeier, "Female Language for God: Should the Church Adopt It?" *The Hermeneutical Quest*, Donald G. Miller, ed. (Allison Park: Pickwick Publications, 1986), pp. 97–114.

PART ONE
THEORETICAL CONSIDERATIONS

Simply stated, an adult female will be naturally transformed into a social mother when she bears a child, but there is no corresponding natural transformation for a male.*

* Peter Wilson, *Man the Promising Primate: The Conditions of Human Evolution*, Second Edition (Yale University Press, 1983), p. 71.

2.

ORIGINS OF THE
FATHER-INVOLVED FAMILY

Due to the marginality of males in the reproductive process, fathering is a cultural acquisition to an extent that mothering is not. Hence, when a culture ceases to support a father's involvement with his own children (through its laws, mores, symbols, models, rituals) powerful natural forces take over in favor of the mother-alone family.

Powerful trends in our culture are calling into question prior traditions regarding fathers.[1] In attacking "patriarchy" and calling for equality of the sexes some feminists appear to want to discredit the significance of gender distinctions altogether.[2] At the same time there is growing alarm over marriage breakdown and the multiplication of single-parent, mother-led families. We are approaching the point, statisticians tell us, when almost half of all North American children will be raised in such essentially fatherless families for some part of their lives.[3]

In reaction, we are witnessing a fresh wave of interest in fathering and the father's role in the emotional development of children.[4] Caught between these conflicting trends many are in a state of confusion. Are fathers important or not? If important, in what sense, and why is it seemingly so difficult for fathers to assume their proper roles in their families as caretakers of children?

One source of our confusion would appear to be the inadequate picture we have of the origins of the "father-involved" family. Contrary to prevailing assumptions "fathering" is not something that can be taken for granted. Neither in the world of antiquity nor today are fathers necessarily the involved, "in charge" figures patriarchal theory portrays them as being—certainly not if by this is meant any significant role in the care and training of their own children.[5] In the myths of the ancient world, for example, it is not the father deities who are thought of as ruling the world, but their wives, sons and daughters.[6] That therefore God should be thought of in biblical faith as involved, gracious, "redemptive" father (Is 63:16) is also not to be taken for granted.[7]

How then *did* the father-involved family originate?

THEORETICAL CONSIDERATIONS

Due to the fragmentary nature of the historical data bearing on this issue, it may be well to begin our discussion of this question with certain theoretical considerations first of all. As a number of researchers have already recognized, an adequate hypothesis in this regard must begin with a recognition of the degree to which fathering is a largely *cultural* acquisition due to the marginality of males in the reproductive process.[8] After sexual intercourse there is no *biologically* compelling reason for the male to have anything further to do with the child he may have engendered. Rather, from the moment of conception onward the growth of the fetus is solely the affair of the female. For nine months it develops in her womb and then is born of her body and suckles at her breasts. A female may choose to abort her child, or abandon it at birth, but if she allows biology to take its course, she will become a mother to her child by an inevitable natural process. Nature does not dictate to the same degree what a male's role shall be in the life of his child.

Looked at from this perspective, it is apparent that for there to be fathering in a *more than* biological sense, a set of overlapping, largely cultural developments were (and are) required.

First, a scientific discovery had to be made. Human beings had to become conscious of the link that exists between a specific act of sexual intercourse and the gestation and birth of a child nine months later.[9] Only when that link had been established could the children born to a certain mother be recognized as belonging to a specific father as well. This recognition must have been slow in coming, since not every sexual act does in fact lead to a pregnancy. Indeed, there are primitive tribes even today yet (or there were just a few years ago), such as the Melanesian Trobrianders described by Malinowski, where this truth has not yet dawned.[10] Among them a woman is thought of as bearing children of herself (once her womb has been opened) through the implantation and reincarnation of departed spirits. This being so, her male companion is not regarded as the father of her children, but as "husband of my mother" (as the children refer to him), or even as "stranger" or "outsider." As a consequence, "between the father and the children there is no union whatsoever," Malinowski writes.[11] Children are regarded instead as belonging exclusively to the mother and her extended family, and in point of fact come into the custody of the mother's brother as they grow older. From this we can see how critical was the discovery of male involvement in reproduction for the formation of father-involved families.

However, even with an awareness of the male's role in pregnancy firmly in place, as we know it was, for example, in the ancient near east, and in Greece, in the second millennium B.C. already,[12] an additional development had to occur for the father-involved family to become an established institution. If a given child is to be recognized as the offspring of a specific male (and not just of the female), bonds are needed between *individual* men and women that are *sexually exclusive*. Only in that way is a given male able to know that the children born to a certain woman are truly *his* and not someone else's. Furthermore, this pair-bonding of male and female must be sufficiently durable to insure that the male involved will be present nine months later when his child is born, not to speak of his availability during the years when his children are growing to maturity. In other words, *psychological* fathering by a child's own father is only possible within a carefully regulated framework of sexual relations between specific men and women extending over the period of time the children are being born and growing to maturity.[13]

But even with this, a given male's actual care of his own children is by no means assured. In addition to knowing *how* children are generated, and in addition to *being there* as they are born and growing up, an equally momentous transformation was required in the *mutual attitudes* of the males and females involved toward these offspring. Now that *two* parents are present instead of one, the females, who until this time had regarded the children born to them as *theirs* exclusively (by virtue of their only too obvious role in their gestation and birth), must now begin to defer to the males, granting them too a share in the ownership of these children. And the males on their part, in spite of being outsiders to the whole birthing process, must also begin now to accept this new role—taking ownership and responsibility and sharing in their children's care.[14]

"Simply stated," writes Wilson, upon whose analysis of these issues I have relied for the prior description,[15]

> an adult female will be naturally transformed into a social mother when she bears a child, but there is no corresponding natural transformation for a male. If he becomes a social father he does so only culturally or symbolically and, as it were, by permission of the female. . . . Only if we bear in mind this meaning of "father" [he adds] and the vulnerability of the father to nature and the female can we explain the dominance of the male/father in all human cultures, which can first be seen in the asymmetry between the relations of mother/offspring and father/offspring.

To summarize: in that a child grows in the body of its mother, mothering is a biologically determined experience to a far greater extent than is fathering. By contrast, fathering is a predominantly cultural acquisition. Its prerequisites are the discovery of the male role in reproduction, the formation of exclusive, enduring sexual bonds between a specific male and female, and their mutual willingness to share in the ownership and care of the children born to them. Seen in this light the emergence of the

father-involved family may be characterized as a truly revolutionary event.

HISTORICAL CONSIDERATIONS

When and how did this revolution occur? As to when, a look
around us at our own culture should convince us that it would be
wrong to say it has even yet occurred. It is still occurring. We are
in the midst of it. The ease with which we have recently adopted
the "new morality" of the sexual revolution and are now prepared, apparently, to live with its consequences (high abortion
rates, epidemic venereal disease, high divorce rates, an enormous
increase in mother-led families where fathers are present hardly
at all) should be evidence enough that the father-involved family
is indeed a recent, still imperfectly realized cultural and spiritual
acquisition.

A glance at our primitive past and the world of the higher
primates confirms this analysis. While the industrial and sexual
revolutions have intensified the problems with fathering in modern societies,[16] a careful study of *most* human cultures will reveal
profound difficulties in this area.[17] And when we look even further back into prehistoric cultures and the world of the higher
primates, this is even more the case. In many primitive societies,
for example, men typically have several wives living in separate
houses who are almost totally responsible for the care of the
children born to them. Only after traumatic puberty rituals are
these children wrenched loose from their maternal environment
and integrated into the world of the fathers.[18] Still further back in
our prehominid past among the higher primates fathering is even
less in evidence, it seems, and among the lower orders of life
almost non-existent.[19]

When and how then *did* fathering begin? The Bible itself
suggests an answer that is remarkably congruent with the find-
ings of modern ethnologists. In Genesis 2:4b–25 the deceptively
childlike story is told of the creation of the first man and woman.
In it we are informed that while the male of our species, Adam,
was created first, he was not happy or complete. Consequently a
search was begun to find him a companion. It was then that the

animals were created, but none was able to assuage his loneliness.
This was the moment, the story declares, when Yahweh-elohim
put Adam to sleep and from his side took a rib and created
woman—and when the man awoke and saw what God had done,
he exclaimed, "This at last is bone of my bones and flesh of my
flesh!" The story concludes with this climactic line: "Therefore a
man leaves his father and his mother and cleaves to his wife, and
they become one flesh" (Gen 2:24).

This text which was quoted approvingly by Jesus (Mk 10:7–
9), and in this way has become the marital ideal of Christianity as
well as Judaism, is a perfectly frank and lucid acknowledgment of
the heightened role that heterosexuality plays among humans as
compared to animals.[20] Among the higher primates heterosexual
relating occurs, for the most part, randomly and sporadically—
only at the specific and often limited time of the female estrus. As a
result sexual intercourse is an impersonal, episodic, socially and
psychologically marginal and inconsequential event. A decisive
step in the direction of psychological fathering occurred when
"woman" was created—that is, with the phasing out of the restricted estrus in women and the emergence of an enlarged capacity for personal sexual bonding on the part of both men and
women. Anthropologist Helen Fisher, on the basis of the discovery of skeletal remains of a family group along the Hadar River of
the Afar Triangle of Ethiopia, believes such bonding may have
occurred (and males were thus incorporated into the female group)
as early as four million years ago.[21] "Yet," she adds, "these males,
lacking an awareness of paternity, had an ancient tendency to
desert their mates. So youngsters still associated their heritage
with mother. But by now the seeds of kinship had been planted."[22]

This insight of both the Bible and modern ethnology not
only highlights the necessity (previously noted) of this type of
bond arising for fathering to occur, but indicates that a uniquely
human sexuality had first to emerge for this to happen. Without
more enduring personal-sexual bonds between individual men
and women there could be no fathering. Without a heightened
capacity for sexual relating there would likely not have arisen that
unique human capacity for forging such bonds.[22]

CONCLUDING COMMENTS

With this in mind one might say that fathering too is of nature to some degree at least—that is, with the rise of a uniquely human capacity for sexual bonding, there was also now a natural incentive for men and women to remain together to care for the children their sexual relations had engendered. However, this pair-bond of mother and father was (and is) notoriously fragile in comparison with the bond between mother and child. In this sense, mothering is far more profoundly nature-determined than is fathering. *Hence, where a culture ceases to support, through its mores, symbols, models, laws and rituals, the sanctity of the sexual bond between a man and his wife and a father's involvement with his own children, powerful natural forces will inevitably take over in favor of the mother-alone family; the fragility of the sexual bond (and the investment of fathers with children) will give way to the strength of the primary bond between mother and child.*

It is in this sense that the father-involved family must be viewed as a cultural artifact, a creation of the human species—some would argue, the definitive cultural artifact that lies at the foundation of all other cultural achievements and most uniquely distinguishes what it means to be human from other forms of life on this planet.[23] Intuitively, in Genesis 2, in its characterization of the advent of woman as partner to man as the crowning act of the creation story, the Bible alludes to this historic development. Only when this had happened could *human* history as such begin.

Notes

1. These trends may be endemic to American culture. In *Prodigals and Pilgrims: The American Revolution against Patriarchal Authority, 1750–1800* (Cambridge: Cambridge University Press, 1982), p. 267, Jay Fliegelman develops the thesis that "the American revolution against patriarchal authority in the second half of the eighteenth century "provided the paradigm by which Americans for the next two hundred years

would understand and set forth the claims of both individual and national independence." See my comments on a related issue in Chapter 10.

2. Typical are Gerder Lerner's comments in her *The Creation of Patriarchy* (New York: Oxford University Press, 1986), p. 238, where she writes that "gender is a set of cultural roles. It is a costume, a mask, a strait-jacket in which men and women dance their unequal dance."

3. According to Benjamin Schlesinger, *One-Parent Families and Their Children in Canadian Society* (The University of Western Ontario, 1979), p. 89, 10 percent of Canadian families are now one-parent families (involving 850,000 children), with 83 percent headed by mothers. The statistics for the United States are: 14 percent one-parent families (involving 11,311,000 children), 84 percent without fathers. George Miller, "Children and the Congress: A Time to Speak Out," in *The American Psychologist*, 38 (January, 1983): 75, writes that "by the end of the decade there is projected to be a 14 percent increase in the number of children under 10. Close to half of these children can expect to live with only one parent at some time during their childhood." According to a report in *Newsweek* (October 1988), p. 67, something like these conditions already exist in Sweden, where there are four divorces for every seven marriages and "last year [1987] for the first time, there were more Swedish children born out of wedlock than to married parents."

4. Regarding this, see especially the authoritative essays (36 in all) in *Father and Child, Developmental and Clinical Perspectives*, ed. by Stanley Cath, et al. (Boston: Little, Brown, 1982).

5. For an earlier discussion of these issues, see my "The Contemporary Fathering Crisis: The Bible and Research Psychology," *The Conrad Grebel Review* (Fall 1983) pp. 21–37 (reprinted in this volume; see Chapter 8).

6. See my "God as Father in the Bible and the Father Image in Several Contemporary Ancient Near Eastern Myths: A Comparison," *Studies in Religion/Sciences Religieuses* 14/3 (Summer 1985): 347–354 (reprinted in this volume; see Chapter 3).

7. The radical centrality of this metaphor in biblical faith is the

theme of my "Depatriarchalizing God in Biblical Interpretation: A Critique," *The Catholic Biblical Quarterly*, 48/4 (October 1986): pp. 609–616 (reprinted in this volume; see Chapter 4).

8. David Bakan, *And They Took Themselves Wives: The Emergence
of Patriarchy in Western Civilization* (San Francisco: Harper &
Row, 1979); Peter Wilson, *Man the Promising Primate: The
Conditions of Human Evolution*, second edition (New Haven
and London: Yale University Press, 1983; first edition, 1980);
Mary O'Brien, *The Politics of Reproduction* (London: Routledge
& Kegan Paul, 1981).

9. O'Brien, *ibid.*, p. 21, calls attention to "the strong historical
tendency" to suppress this discovery and see reproduction
instead as " 'pure' biological process . . . without mind; irra-
tional or at least prerational."

10. See Bronislaw Malinowski, *The Father in Primitive Psychology*
(New York: W. W. Norton, 1927).

11. Malinowski, *ibid.*, p. 12.

12. Data bearing on this discovery is assembled by David Mace,
Hebrew Marriage: A Sociological Study (London: The Epworth
Press, 1953), pp. 205–206; Gerda Lerner, *The Creation of
Patriarchy*, pp. 185–193; and Mary Lefkowitz and Maureen
Fant, *Women's Life in Greece & Rome: A Source Book in Transla-
tion* (Baltimore: Johns Hopkins University Press, 1982), pp.
82–87. See also the analysis in Chapter 3 below.

13. Gerda Lerner, in her erudite *The Creation of Patriarchy* (New
York: Oxford University Press, 1986), refers to this development as the "appropriation by men of woman's sexual and
reproductive capacity" (p. 8), and regards it as the key event
in the rise of patriarchy (male domination of women). She
does not seem to recognize that this step was essential to the
emergence of the father-involved family as such.

14. Bakan, *And They Took Themselves Wives*, p. 14, refers to this as
the "effeminization of the male. In coming to share the care
of children, he came to share in the archaic function of the
female."

15. Peter Wilson, *Man the Promising Primate*, p. 71.

16. Regarding these modern developments, see especially Alex-

ander Mitscherlich, *Society without the Father: A Contribution to Social Psychology* (New York: Harcourt, Brace & World, 1963; English translation, 1969), and Edward Shorter, *The Making of the Modern Family* (New York: Basic Books, Inc., 1975).

17. The way, for example, the typical Greek father of antiquity neglected his wife and children (and the consequences of this) are fully documented by Philip Slater, *The Glory of Hera: Greek Mythology and the Greek Family* (Boston: Beacon Press, 1968); for similar problems in African society, see H. Collomb and S. Valantin, "The Black African Family," in J. Anthony and C. Koupernik, eds., *The Child in His Family* (New York: J. Wiley, 1970), pp. 359–388; for India, see Sudhir Kakar, "Father and Sons: An Indian Experience," in Stanley Cath, et al., eds., *Father and Child* (Boston: Little, Brown, 1982), pp. 417–442; for China, Japan, and other examples, see the summaries in David Lynn, *The Father*, pp. 33–44.

18. Regarding the severity of these rituals as this relates to the intensity of the mothering factor and the non-involvement of the fathers, see William N. Stephens, *The Oedipus Complex: Cross-Cultural Evidence* (New York: The Free Press of Glencoe, 1962).

19. The evidence bearing on fathering among the prehominid primates is summarized by Wilson, *Man the Promising Primate*, who states, that "on the whole it can be said that most primate males are unable to identify their children" (p. 48). Foreshadowings of a fathering role appear in a few lower species (wolves and gibbons are the notable examples); its absence, and the dominance instead of the mother among virtually all other sentient animals (and generally among primitive cultures) is thoroughly documented by Robert Biffault, *The Mothers: The Matriarchal Theory of Social Origins* (New York: Macmillan, 1931).

20. "The myth breathes an atmosphere of unabashed sensuality," writes Samuel Terrien of this passage, in *Till the Heart Sings: A Biblical Theology of Manhood & Womanhood* (Philadelphia: Fortress Press, 1986), p. 16.

21. Helen Fisher, *The Sex Contract, The Evolution of Human Behavior* (New York: Quill, 1982), pp. 121f.
22. *Ibid.*, p. 145.
23. The complex nature of this achievement is the central theme of Wilson's *Man the Promising Primate*.

3

MALE-CENTERED REPRODUCTIVE BIOLOGY AND THE DYNAMICS OF BIBLICAL PATRIARCHY

The discovery (as it was thought) that life originates in male semen had a revolutionary impact on the form of the family in the cultures of the ancient near east. It not only solidified the role of fathers in families, but increased the potential for wife and child abuse. However, steps were taken early on to curtail such abuse both outside and within biblical culture.

The family histories in Genesis which trace the origins of peoples, including the biblical people, reflect a quite specific stage in the emergence of the father-involved family in the ancient near east during the third and second millennia B.C. The families of this period and region are now generally regarded as "patriarchal," which literally translated refers to the father (*pater*) as "beginning" or "first" (*arche*) and to the tracing of lineage through the male line. Once a title of honor (Acts 2:27) "patriarch" has more recently come to be viewed in a negative light as signifying an *excess* or abuse of male prerogative and power.

What I wish to indicate in this essay, however, is that the patriarchy of this era, when viewed from the perspective of the conditions essential to a male's involvement in family life, may be judged to have had both a negative *and* positive side to it, and that especially in that cycle of stories, beginning with Genesis 12, that informs us of the origins of the biblical people, testimony is given to a momentous break with certain darker aspects of the patriarchal heritage of that region and period at one very crucial point: in the story of Abraham's near-sacrifice of his son Isaac (Gen 22:1–18) the legitimacy of a father's right to kill his own child is directly spoken to and challenged for the first time in history, so far as we know.

In order to appreciate what was involved in this breakthrough, and how important it was, it will be necessary first of all, however, to take a careful look at the cultural framework which allowed fathers to have such absolute power over their children in the first place. A primary factor in this development appears to have been the discovery of the male role in a child's conception. An analysis of this matter will not only afford us insights into the dynamics of ancient near eastern patriarchy, but assist us in appreciating what it meant for the biblical people to challenge, moderate and utilize this cultural setting for the advances in father-involvement that would follow.

REPRODUCTIVE THEORY

The conception of a child was a mysterious event for the peoples of antiquity. "I do not know how you appeared in my womb," testifies the mother of the seven Maccabaean martyrs (2 Mac 7:22). "You do not understand how the wind blows, or how the embryo grows in a woman's womb," writes the venerable Qoheleth; "no more can you understand the work of God, the Creator of all" (Eccl 11:5 *New Jerusalem Bible*). An aspect of this mystery was the sexual act itself. Its connection with pregnancy and the birth of a child nine months later was by no means apparent. Indeed, it is not improbable that the earliest thinking regarding pregnancy and birth bypassed the male involvement altogether and regarded women as generating children *by themselves* with the help of God. This appears to be the context within which the veneration of the mother-goddess in the Neolithic and Chalcolithic periods proliferated.[1]

The reproductive theory that replaced this one in the ancient near east as early as the third millennium B.C. is most clearly spelled out in the works of the fourth century Athenian philosopher, Aristotle. In a rather lengthy essay entitled "The Generation of Animals," he draws a distinction between male and female on the basis of the fluids they emit: menstrual fluid in the case of the female, semen in males. It follows, he writes, that "Male is that which is able to concoct, to cause to take shape, and to discharge semen possessing the 'principle' of the 'form'," whereas "female is that which receives semen, but is unable to cause semen to take shape or discharge it."[2]

What this suggests is an understanding of the reproductive process that is almost the opposite of the earlier point of view. Far from the mother being thought of as primary (or even sole) source of the child she bears, it is the male now who is viewed as producing that which is essential to the creation of children. The consequences of this new understanding for family law, Gerda Lerner has noted in her book *The Creation of Patriarchy*, are spelled out in "The Furies," the last play in the "Oresteia" trilogy by Aeschylus, where the playright lets Apollo settle an argument over mother-right by declaring:[3]

> The mother is not the parent of the child
> which is called hers. She is the nurse who tends
> the growth
> Of young seed planted by its true parent,
> the male.

The likening of semen to seed in this passage is one that reappears with some frequency in biblical sources. Thus Abraham is told that "Your heir will be the issue [semen] of your own body" (Gen 15:4). Subsequently, Abraham was led outside, shown the stars, and promised: "Just so will your seed be" (15:5, 18). Thus, in exact accordance with Aristotelian reproductive biology, Isaac is here regarded as coming forth from his *father's* body (not his mother's).

If male sexual discharge is now regarded as "seed," it follows that the female womb is understood as "ground" of sorts into which the seed is planted. Job 10:10–11 likens semen to a substance that was poured out "like milk," then allowed to "thicken like curds" (in the womb), at which point it was then clothed with skin and flesh and woven with bone and sinew (see also Ps 139:13). A similar picture of conception is drawn in the first century B.C. book of Wisdom, where King Solomon is quoted as saying:

> I was modelled in flesh inside a mother's womb,
> where, for ten [lunar] months, in blood I acquired substance—
> the result of virile seed and pleasure,
> sleep's companion (Wis 7:1–2. *New Jerusalem Bible*).

The first century B.C. Jewish philosopher Philo echoes this conception when he writes:[4]

> Now seed is the original starting-point of living creatures. That this is a substance of a very low order, resembling foam, is evident to the eye. But when it has been deposited in the womb and become solid, it acquires movement, and at once enters upon natural growth.

In this pre-scientific biology "there is of course no thought of the part played by the ovum," David Mace observes. "The new individual is fashioned solely out of the impregnating principle provided by the father, at the behest of Yahweh. . . . The womb of the mother simply constitutes the receptacle within which God works His mysterious miracle."[5] The persistence of such reproductive concepts in middle eastern culture down to modern times is indicated by a reference in the eighth century Koran to a child being fashioned by Alla from a "sperm drop" (Sura XVIII: 37).

David Mace has noted how consistent this reproductive view is with the biblical principle of patriarchal succession from father to son, for if children originate in the "seed" of the *father*, then "the continuity of the 'line' can logically exist only through the males of the family," and the particular woman who happens to bear sons to a man is from the point of view of succession a matter of indifference; hence the complete absence in Hebrew thought of our modern conceptions of 'legitimacy.' The woman supplies nothing of her essential self to the new being. She merely provides in her womb the human incubator in which the man's seed becomes his child, the reproduction of his image.[6]

More might be said, but from the data already surveyed it seems evident that a quite specific set of pre-scientific biological concepts contributed to the emergence and shape of that unique form of father involvement that prevailed in the ancient near east during the third and second millennia B.C.

AN ASSESSMENT

What needs to be evaluated, however, is what the social consequences of this were and are. Two quite contrasting assessments of this development have been put forward by researchers to date. The Canadian psychologist David Bakan, for example, appears to regard it as essentially a positive one in that it enabled men in particular to overcome what he terms a "crisis of paternalization"—that is, the generic reluctance among males to involve themselves in the ownership and care of their own children. "If the seed is that of the male, if it is his property," he writes, "then it is essential to develop social methods of guaranteeing female fidelity in marriage and virginity prior to marriage," in order to guarantee "that the offspring of the female are the offspring of the male." Then too the male will begin assuming "obligations of maintenance, protection, and education of the offspring, which prior to this have been associated with the female."[7]

The feminist historian Gerda Lerner evaluates this same set of events quite differently. In the wake of the discovery of the male role in reproduction, she writes, there did indeed occur a development in which men came to have exclusive rights to the sexuality of certain females, but in making themselves subservient sexually in this manner, women lost their autonomy and became subordinate to males as a group, and children too came under the autocratic authority of the father.[8] In fact, Lerner argues, here lie the origins of that excessive patriarchalism that remains to this day such a blight on the world. Thus, only as women take back ownership and control of their sexuality, she insists, will they achieve the strength, identity and autonomy needed to move beyond patriarchy and rectify its abuses.[9] Erudite and detailed as her analysis is, however, she does not tell us how this can be done without bringing to an end the involvement of men in fathering their own children.[10]

There is truth, it seems, in both of these assessments. If the reproductive biology outlined above did not recognize sufficiently the genetic contributions of the female to the child she bore, looked at in the light of the conditions necessary for fathering (knowledge of the male role in reproduction, and an enduring and exclusive bond on the part of the male with a female partner),[11] it must be judged a valuable development insofar as it strengthened the heretofore fragile relations of men to their wives and offspring, and in this way gave rise to a particularly solid and tenacious form of father-involvement in the reproduction of the species. With the procreational biology outlined above in place, any questions as to a father's rightful share in the fruit of his wife's womb were swept aside. While the child was still obviously the mother's in that her body provided the indispensable matrix for its gestation and growth, it was clearly also now the father's as well (and peculiarly so), in that it originated in his body from his semen.

I concur therefore with Bakan that the general impact of this reproductive concept (flawed though it was) was a positive one. It helped males overcome a species-wide developmental crisis in paternalization, and provided a solid foundation for the emergence of fathering as a distinctively human characteristic.

Nevertheless, it must also be acknowledged (in agreement with Lerner) that this biological perspective could and did contribute to the emergence of exaggerated notions of paternal power and authority in the nuclear family, which, if unregulated, could (and did) result in abuses on the father's part against other members of his family. In what follows I will try to indicate that the potential for *wife abuse* under these circumstances was already long recognized in ancient near eastern culture prior to the rise of biblical culture, and that steps had been taken to protect against this. Unfortunately, the same cannot be said regarding the potential for *child abuse*. Abuse of children was all too commonplace in the ancient near east, including their outright slaughter. It is precisely for this reason that the stories that open the biblical record, particularly the account in Genesis 22 that tells of Abraham's break with the prevailing notions of child sacrifice, are of such great significance for the future of the father-involved family.

1. Protection Against Wife Abuse

With the advent of a biology that understood the male sexual affluent as the point of origin of a child, fidelity in sexual relations became imperative. While male-female sexual bonding had been a distinctive human trait long prior to this (see the discussion of this point in Chapter 2), the importance now attaching to the *exclusivity* of such bonds became suddenly and dramatically apparent. Only if a given male had sole and exclusive rights to a specific female's womb could he be certain that the children born to her would be his and not someone else's. Consequently, in all ancient near eastern law codes, including the biblical codes, adultery (sexual relations between a man's wife and a male other than her husband) is regarded as a crime punishable by death (see, for example, Code of Hammurabi 129; Lev 20:10).

This stipulation, however (that a wife's sexuality belongs exclusively to her husband), could have as one of its consequences that the husband might begin thinking of his wife as a possession to do with as he pleased. As just noted, however, *this* category of problem was recognized and addressed quite early in the ancient near east. In the eighteenth century B.C. Code of Hammurabi (CH), for example, there is a large section devoted to possible points of contention of the partners in a marriage regarding their mutual and individual rights (see laws 128–195), and even a cursory reading of these texts will indicate how then, already, the distinctions were drawn between marital-sexual rights, on the one hand, and the rights of husbands and wives *as persons*, on the other. No more was a *wife* regarded as her husband's possession to do with as he pleased than was *he* regarded as the wife's possession to do with as she pleased. *Both* parties to a marriage needed protection from abuse by the other, these laws imply, but the larger number of laws devoted to the rights of wives does suggest that women especially were vulnerable to abuse and in need of help at this point. However, such help was forthcoming, it seems, in the legal traditions of this region.[12]

A husband, for example, was not permitted to sell his wife into slavery. Nor is there any hint of a privileged position on his part that would excuse him for physically abusing her. The worst that a man could do to a wife who displeased him (or failed to bear him a child) was to divorce her; even then, however (according to the Code of Hammurabi), he had to give her "the full amount of her marriage price" (the sum of money he had given her father in compensation at the time of marriage), plus the dowry she had brought with her into the marriage (CH 138). The Hammurabi Code also permits a wife to leave her husband should she come to hate him, and if upon investigation her displeasure was shown to be justified, she could even take her dowry with her (CH 142). Even a woman who humiliates and neglects her husband, due to her too many business activities outside the home, is not punished on this account, except that her husband was then permitted to marry a second wife, and her status in the home was reduced to that of a maidservant (CH 141).

It should also be kept in mind that marriages in this culture were not the affair of two people only, but of their families, clans and villages, and were in this way monitored for potential abuses and injustices by a wider community. The very ancient practice of a compensatory payment to the wife's family by the bridegroom is but one example of this wider accountability of the marital couple, as is the wife's family's provision of a dowry for their daughter—that is, a sum of wealth which was hers to keep as her own even after she moved into her husband's house. This latter (her dowry) may be regarded as her family's attempt at providing her with at least some economic self-sufficiency, even though married.

Biblical culture and law reflect these traditions. There too a dowry was customary (Gen 31:14–16), it seems, and a man's free-born wife was clearly not her husband's possession to do with as he pleased.[13] He did not own her as one owns a slave (unless, of course, she was in fact a slave-wife). In biblical law too the worst thing he might do, should she displease him, would be to divorce her, at which point she was free to marry someone else (see Dt 24:1–3).

This is not to deny, however, that even in this area there were ongoing problems of a subtler kind that continued to plague this relationship (and still do). While heightening the importance of virginity and fidelity (a sine qua non if men were to know who their children were), the new awareness of the male role in reproduction did not similarly clarify the issue of *how many* wives a man might have. Nor did it lead at once to a resolution of what attitude should be taken toward prostitution, sacred or otherwise. Also, in a culture where slavery was still widespread, there were issues to contend with regarding the incorporation of slave wives into a man's household.

Even a glance at biblical narrative and law will indicate the degree to which issues of this kind remained problematic almost to the end of the biblical period. Thus, the founder of the biblical people, Abraham, is portrayed in Genesis as taking to wife not just Sarah, but her slave girl (Gen 16), and Abraham's grandson, Jacob, inadvertently becomes the husband of two wives, not just one (Gen 29). In another ancient story, Judah, forefather of the tribe of Judah, is said to have had intercourse with someone he thought to be a prostitute, but whom he later learned was his daughter-in-law (Gen 38). The practice of having slaves for wives, and a plurality of wives, is implied in Israel's oldest law code (Ex 21:7–11). Later on Israel's greatest king, David, took to himself numerous wives and concubines (2 Sam 5:13).

Only gradually, it seems, did there emerge within human culture generally, and within biblical culture specifically, the recognition that the monogamous fidelity required of a wife is the ideal for husbands as well (see the admonitions in this regard in Gen 2:22–25; Prv 5; 7:6–27; Mal 2:13–16; Mk 10:1–12), and that random sexual relations apart from a marital intent (prostitution) are dehumanizing (Hos 4:14; Prv 29:3; I Cor 6:15f).

2. The Vulnerability of Children

The other relation both positively and negatively affected by the advent of male-centered reproductive biology was that of the father's relation to his children. The impact of the new biological understandings in *this* regard, it seems, was even greater than its impact on wife-husband relations, for men and women had been *sexually* bonding for millennia prior to the advent of a specific reproductive theory that ascribed procreativity to the male.[14] So far as that relationship was concerned, therefore, an androcentric reproductive concept simply added to the significance of this bond and further strengthened it by accenting how important was the male contribution to the reproductive process. However, the impact of this new biological understanding upon how the children themselves were now viewed must have been nothing short of revolutionary, for prior to this children were regarded as belonging exclusively to the mother (in that they were thought to have originated solely from her), whereas now they were viewed as originating solely from the father.

It was this dramatic reversal of perspective, we may conjecture, that laid the foundation for the famous *patria potestas* (power of the father) which in ancient Roman culture reached its zenith in fathers being given the right by law even to kill their children, should they wish to do so.[15] Coming as it did from his loins, the child was now thought of as belonging to the father to do with as he wished. Indeed, in Babylonian law children were so much linked to the father that sons could be punished for their father's crimes. Even in biblical law a striking difference can be noted between the authority a father had over his children in comparison to his authority over his wife. As noted, he was *not* permitted to sell his wife into slavery; she was not his property to dispose of as he wished. But he *was* permitted to sell his children (see, for example, Ex 21:7). Was he also permitted to *kill* them (as were Roman fathers of antiquity)?

These questions are crucially important ones for assessing the impact of biblical faith on the prevailing culture of fathering, and for sensing how at this point too it began forging a new way. However, to gain a proper appreciation of the significance of these developments, it will be necessary to digress a bit and note how pervasive in antiquity was the practice of killing children, and also how deep-seated were the rationalizations for doing so.

INFANTICIDE AND CHILD SACRIFICE

One of the most gruesome consequences of the notion that a father owned his children (because of their having originated from his body) was the practice of infanticide and child sacrifice in the cultures of antiquity. This is a skeleton in the closet of humanity that dare not be ignored if we are to grasp the severity of the problems that even today yet must be surmounted if we are ever to be successful in civilizing the father-involved family.

Since the literature on this subject is extensive (and can be readily consulted by anyone interested in knowing more about it), I will confine myself here to a few examples only.[16] In ancient Rome children at birth were regularly laid at their father's feet for his decision as to whether they should live or die. If he lifted them up, they would live; if left on the ground, they would be taken away and exposed to die in some predetermined place. It was from this pool of abandoned children that the slaves and prostitutes of ancient cultures were often drawn.

So widespread was infanticide in ancient Greece that the historians of antiquity saw it as the chief reason for the decline of Hellenistic culture. But not only among the Greeks and Romans were such practices rife—all over the Mediterranean region in this period infanticide and child sacrifice were rampant. Of the Carthaginians Plutarch wrote (in his *De superstitione*) that they slew their children "as if they were lambs or chickens. . . . They placed them one by one, on the sloping hands of the brazen image, from which they rolled into the pit of fire. . . . The mothers had to stand by and see it done without a tear or groan."

The Bible itself testifies to the prevalence of such gruesome rituals. 2 Kings 3:26–27, for example, tells of a Moabite king who sacrificed his son, and Deuteronomy 12:31 indicates that practices of this kind were also common among the Canaanites. Indeed, even Israelite fathers, we are told, did such things too from time to time (see Jer 7:31–34; 19:5–25; 32:35–36); at least two Israelite kings are said to have sacrificed their first-born sons (2 Kgs 16:3; 21:6. See also 1 Kgs 16:34).

Why? What motivated fathers to slaughter their own children in this seemingly senseless manner? In seeking an answer, one notes, to begin with, the assumption that they had the right to do so. Nowhere in the cultures of antiquity outside of Israel was this right challenged, so far as we know. The rationalizations for such conduct were, as a result, free to proliferate and could be quite varied, it seems. *Religious* motives predominated in some instances. For example, if animal sacrifices were efficacious for the atonement of sins, it was imagined, how much more the sacrifice of one's own children, and one's first-born above all!

> With what shall I enter Yahweh's presence
> and bow down before God All-high?
> Shall I enter with burnt offerings,
> with calves one year old?
> Will he be pleased with rams by the thousand,
> with ten thousand streams of oil?
> Shall I offer my eldest son for my wrong-doing,
> the child of my own body for my sin?
> (Mic 6:6–7. *New Jerusalem Bible*).

In other instances children were killed simply as a means of birth control, much as today abortion is practiced. A letter written in 1 B.C. by an Egyptian migrant laborer named Hilarion, to his wife, Alis, pregnant with his second child, advises her, "If by chance you bear a child, if it is a boy, let it be; if it is a girl, cast it out . . ." (*Papyrus Oxyrhynchus* 744). More complex psychological dynamics, such as paternal irritation, fear, or hatred, could also be involved. In a famous creation myth from Mesopotamia the father-deity, Apsu, is characterized as so maddened by the noisiness of his offspring that he determined to kill them to keep them from disturbing his sleep! Such trivial paternal irritations might be intensi-

fied by alliances between children and their mothers against the
fathers. Such is the theme of the biblical story of the collusion of
Rebekah and Jacob against Isaac (Gen 27), a tale reminiscent of the
Oedipus Rex legends of Greece. In these latter a son, abandoned
by his father, inadvertently murders him and marries his mother.
In certain primitive cultures, paternal dread of something like this
happening was so great that a ritual funeral for the father was
enacted during his wife's pregnancy. For similar reasons first-born
Ugandan sons were, until recently, choked to death by attending
midwives with the father's implicit permission.

From all this it is apparent that if the advent of the father-
involved family brought blessing, it also brought turmoil and
tragedy. Not just one but *two* people were now intimately involved in *shared* ownership and care of the children born to them.
Prior to this a child belonged to the mother alone, and her maternal instincts helped to guarantee its protection and care. But now
that a father was also present—now that it was understood that
the child belonged to him as well (and not just to the mother)—
would *he also* protect and nurture it with a degree of love and
concern that matched hers? Would he also, *as father*, be mother-
like to his children, and truly care for them?

INTIMATIONS OF ANOTHER WAY: GENESIS 22

Just as we can trace a development within biblical culture
corrective of some of the possible abuses of spouses toward one
another (and in the direction of monogamy and marital fidelity on
the part of women *and* men), so we can also identify developments there in the direction of greater protection of children.
Such, I suggest, is the significance of that moving account that
stands at the apex and conclusion of the Abraham stories in Genesis: the one in Genesis 22 that relates the gripping episode of
Abraham's near-sacrifice of his only son Isaac. This particular
story opens with a command from God to Abraham to sacrifice
his son, a command which Abraham sets out to obey *only too
willingly*, it seems. At the critical moment, however, his hand is
stayed, and he is ordered not to harm his son after all, for what
God wanted, we learn, was not *Isaac's* actual sacrifice, but some-

thing from *Abraham*—his inner awe and respect, and that only (Gen 22:12).

Although not legislation in the strict sense of the word, the commandment from heaven at this story's climactic conclusion *not to kill his son or do him any harm* (Gen 22:12) is the first definitive declaration we know of delimiting the authority of a father over his children and prohibiting him from taking his child's life.[17] As such, this narrative may be regarded as a first charter of children's rights (see the essay in the Appendix for a fuller exposition of this text from this perspective). Only when this point had been clarified (that fathers must not arbitrarily kill or harm their children for any reason) could a culture of fatherhood begin to flourish, as it subsequently did in biblical tradition.[18]

SUMMARY

An especially tenacious form of father-involved family came to birth in the ancient near east in the wake of the discovery of the male role in reproduction. This discovery had a twofold impact: it consolidated paternal consciousness and the rights of fathers to exclusive sexual access to specific women and to their own children (codified in a growing body of laws and customs in support of marital fidelity); at the same time, wives and children became more vulnerable to abuse of paternal authority.

Potential abuses of wives (or husbands) within the marital relationship were already identified and dealt with in the marital laws and traditions of the ancient near east generally. In this regard biblical tradition at the beginning simply reflected its wider cultural background. On the other hand, biblical faith would early on become innovative in the face of child abuse. As the story of Abraham's near sacrifice of his only son Isaac so powerfully intimates, already the patriarchs of the Bible began to break with their culture at one very crucial point: they came to see that the sacrificial slaughter of children by their fathers was not what God wanted.

Notes

1. Gerda Lerner, *The Creation of Patriarchy* (New York: Oxford University Press, 1986), pp. 146–152; David Bakan, *And They Took Themselves Wives: The Emergence of Patriarchy in Western Civilization* (San Francisco: Harper & Row, 1979), p. 26; Ann Barstow, "The Prehistoric Goddess," in *The Book of the Goddess Past and Present: An Introduction to Her Religion*, Carl Olson, ed. (New York: Crossroad, 1985), pp. 7–15.

2. Quoted from Mary R. Lefkowitz and Maureen B. Fant, *Women's Life in Greece & Rome: A Source Book in Translation* (Baltimore: Johns Hopkins University Press, 1982), p. 84.

3. Lerner, *Creation of Patriarchy*, p. 205.

4. *De Opificio Mundi*, 67, quoted from Ephraim Urbach, *The Sages* (Cambridge: Harvard University Press, 1987), p. 226.

5. David Mace, *Hebrew Marriage: A Sociological Study* (London: The Epworth Press, 1953), p. 206.

6. *Ibid.*

7. David Bakan, *They Took Themselves Wives*, pp. 27f.

8. "Thus," she writes, "the first appropriation of private property consists of the appropriation of the labor of women as *reproducers.*" Gerda Lerner, *Creation of Patriarchy*, p. 52.

9. *Ibid.*, p. 218.

10. "What will come after," she concludes, "what kind of structure will be the foundation for alternate forms of social organization we cannot yet know." *Ibid.*, p. 229.

11. See "Origins of the Father-Involved Family" (Chapter 2 in this volume).

12. For a review of family law in the Hammurabi Code and the Bible, see Hans Jochen Boecker, *Law and the Administration of Justice in the Old Testament and the Ancient East* (Minneapolis: Augsburg, 1980), pp. 100–122.

13. For a nuanced discussion of this point, see the definitive study of Israelite marriage customs and ceremonies by David Mace, *Hebrew Marriage: A Sociological Study* (London: The Epworth Press, 1953), pp. 189–200.

14. See Helen E. Fisher, *The Sex Contract: The Evolution of Human Behavior* (New York: Quill, 1983), pp. 119–122, for fossil

evidence of male participation in the family group as early as four million years ago.

15. For a summary of the Roman traditions and laws in this regard, see "The *Patria Potestas*," in William Barclay, *Train Up a Child* (Philadelphia: Westminster, 1959), pp. 267–270.

16. For a review of this tragic chapter of our human past (and the shadow it continues to cast over our present), see Erich Wellisch's book-length study, *Isaac and Oedipus. A Study in Biblical Psychology of the Sacrifice of Isaac: The Akedah* (Routledge & Kegan Paul, 1953); Michael Tooley, *Abortion and Infanticide* (Oxford: Clarendon Press, 1983); Alberto Ravinell and Whitney Green, *The Role of Human Sacrifice in the Ancient Near East* (Missoula: Scholars Press, 1975); Bernhard Erling, "First-Born and Firstlings in the Covenant Code," *Society of Biblical Literature Seminar Papers Series*, No. 25 (Atlanta: Scholars Press, 1986), pp. 470–490.

17. Wellisch's study, *Isaac and Oedipus*, highlights the importance of this event for the future of the father-involved family.

18. The way a high culture of fathering flourished within the context of biblical faith, and why, is the focus of the essays in Parts III and IV of this volume.

PART TWO

GOD AS FATHER IN BIBLICAL TRADITION

The God of Judaism is undoubtedly a father-symbol and father-image, possibly the greatest such symbol and image conceived by man. Nor can there be any doubt as to the psychological need answered by this image. This, together with the great moral imperatives, was the unique contribution of prophetic Judaism to mankind.*

* Raphael Patai, *The Hebrew Goddess* (New York: Avon Books, 1967), p. 9.

4.

GOD AS FATHER IN THE BIBLE AND THE FATHER IMAGE IN SEVERAL CONTEMPORARY ANCIENT NEAR EASTERN MYTHS: A COMPARISON

The assumption that biblical father religion is simply continuous with wider ancient near eastern patriarchalism is unsupported by a comparison of the portrait of God as father in the Bible with divine father figures in several contemporary ancient near eastern mythologies. Only in biblical tradition is it believed that a father-god truly worthy of being hallowed is fully in charge of the cosmic home.

If, as has been argued, myths like dreams are "symbolic of the dynamics of the psyche,"[1] and "modal familial experiences . . . play an important part in shaping the fantasy products of a culture,"[2] it would appear that the peoples of the ancient near east during the second millennium B.C. were experiencing a fathering crisis of sorts. In many of their myths, in any case, fathers present problems. Their marginality, cruelty, incompetence, or powerlessness, more often than not, poses dilemmas to which mother, son or daughter deities must respond either by defending themselves or by taking action to uphold the universe in their stead.[3] Only in biblical myth, it seems, is there a divine father who is a major force for good in the life of the world. This raises the question whether biblical faith in God as father, often said to

43

reflect an already established patriarchal order, may not instead have arisen on the wings of an emotional revolution.[4]

My purpose in this essay is not, however, primarily to search out how or why this happened, but simply to highlight a few of the more important comparisons and contrasts that can be drawn when looking at the portrait of God as father in the Bible against the backdrop of divine father images in several contemporary myths of the ancient near east. Three mythologies in particular outside the Bible stand out as characteristic of religious imagination in that region during this period: the Babylonian creation story, Enuma Elis, the Canaanite Baal poems from Ugarit, and the Egyptian tale of Osiris and Isis. After reviewing each of these briefly, I will turn to the biblical myth and then conclude with a few thoughts regarding the significance of the comparisons that emerge.

ENUMA ELIS

Religion in second millennium B.C. Mesopotamia was characterized by a large number of nature deities thought to be organized into a divine state. They are also represented in the myths as a divine family, the dynamics of which are most fully revealed in the Babylonian creation story, Enuma Elis.[5]

Two crises marked the coming into being of the world as we know it, according to this myth, both precipitated in part by conduct attributed to fathers. At the beginning of creation, the Enuma Elis tells us, there existed only commingling salt and fresh waters conceived of as two parental deities, Tiamat, the mother, and Apsu, the father (I, 1–5). In their midst the younger gods were born: Lahmu and Lahamu, Anshar and Kishar (silt-gods), Anu (the sky-god), and the earth-god Nudimmud or Ea (I, 6–20). The birth of these children, however, brought little joy to their parents, for they were boisterous and loud and disturbed their sleep, so much so that something had to be done. And it was father Apsu, we are told, who hit upon a bold idea. The children should be killed (I, 20–40)! Mother Tiamat, however, upon hearing of this solution, was, to say the least, less than enthusiastic and pleaded with her husband to have patience (I, 40–43). Father

Apsu, however, was in no mood to be dissuaded. His face "radiant" (the text says), he set about executing his murderous plan. But before he could accomplish it, word of his intentions was leaked to his son Ea, who promptly cast a spell over him, putting him to sleep (I, 64). He then proceeded to divest his father of the emblems of his authority (band, tiara, halo), bound him and murdered him (I, 69), after which he built himself a chamber in the midst of the corpse (I, 71–77). With this the curtain is drawn on Act I of the Enuma Elis.

Needless to say the drama to this point has portrayed a family in considerable disarray. The father especially is characterized as a brutish figure at odds with his wife and irritated by his children to the point of wanting to kill them. The children survive by murdering him instead. Thus were the foundations laid for our cosmic home!

A second chapter in the drama of creation begins when Ea, fresh from murdering his father, marries and has a son of his own, the storm-god Marduk (I, 79–84). With Marduk's entry into the story a contest begins to take shape between two groups of gods, those in league with mother Tiamat, now a widow, and those associated with the younger generation of gods under the leadership of sky-god Anshar. Mother Tiamat, it turns out, in the aftermath of her husband's death, was persuaded to do what she had earlier pleaded with him not to do: murder her children (I, 111–117). With this in mind she began fashioning an army of monsters and elevated one of them, Kingu, as commander in chief (I, 125–161).

The crisis that now unfolds is portrayed in the myth as the most severe in the entire history of cosmogenesis (II, 1–48). Who is going to stop mother Tiamat from attacking and destroying her own children and with them the world-home they have succeeded in creating for themselves? The sky-god Anshar, himself now an exalted father deity (Apsu being dead), would appear to be the logical candidate. But Anshar, we are told, upon hearing of the frightful things mother Tiamat was planning to do, shrunk back in fear (II, 50) and turned for assistance to two father deities next in rank, Anu and Ea. But they too were as fearful as he (II, 53–87). Collectively helpless, the divine elders summoned an assembly of the gods, and there it was that the solution to this crisis was arrived at (II, 88–99). What the fathers were too frightened to do, individually or collectively, was laid on the shoulders of the youthful Marduk, and he responded magnificently, it is said, but only after shrewdly exacting a pledge that he would reign as king of the universe in his father's place (II, 122–129). Then without anyone's help he faced the terrible Tiamat, distended and destroyed her, and fashioned the universe out of the remains of her body (IV, 90–145). The myth closes with Marduk completing creation (V–VI, 44) and being given a temple at which were recited his fifty glorious names (VI, 45–VII, 144).

It is not fathers then who rule the universe in the Babylonian vision of reality, but sons, and they rule not with them, but in spite of them. Fathers, it is implied, can be cruel and weak. Sons must defend themselves against them and rise above them. Mothers also can be harsh and destructive and bring terror to both fathers and sons. Then too sons must be resourceful and courageous and not expect their fathers to help them. From this myth we might conjecture that Mesopotamian society was characterized by ambitious, bellicose sons and weak fathers—a configuration, interestingly enough, that recurs in the Gilgamesh Epic, a popular Mesopotamian narrative roughly contemporary in time with the Enuma Elis. In it we read of the journey to maturity of a famous king. His growing up, it turns out, was exceptionally long and tortuous for the very reason that in his case too the fathers were frightened and weak and unable to discipline or guide him, so that he had to find his way pretty much on his own, through trial and error, except for the help of a peer.[6]

THE BAAL MYTHS

Our picture of second millennium Canaanite mythology has been significantly enhanced through the discovery of tablets in the library of the chief priest of the storm god Baal in the ancient city of Ugarit, among which are several that relate Baal's ascent to divine kingship.[7] Baal's father El is creator and titular ruler of the universe. In reality, like the father gods of Mesopotamia, El plays a peculiarly weak and inept role in the life of the world. Three episodes in particular bring this out.

In what is generally regarded as one of the major episodes of the opening drama of this myth the gods are shown assembling at the home of El in the far north (III AB B). Baal is standing at his father's side when messengers arrive from Yam-Nahar (Sea-River) demanding of the assembly and of El that Baal be handed over to them. Apparently they wish to destroy him and inundate the land over which he presides. Their challenge is thus a similar one to that posed by Tiamat in the Enuma Elis. In this instance, however, Sea-River is not thought of as the primeval mother, but as another son in the family of El. In any case, El and his assembly appear to be just as powerless to deal with the challenge as were their Mesopotamian counterparts. To our surprise, in fact, El accedes to the wishes of Yam-Nahar (either out of fear or because he favored Yam-Nahar in the first place). But Baal is quite prepared to take matters into his own hands. Ignoring his father, with the help of a divine craftsman, he sets about clubbing Yam-Nahar into submission (III AB A). In this myth the son not only rises above the weak father to rule the world (as in Mesopotamia), but does so in the face of his father's pathetic willingness to let him be destroyed.

There follows the story of how, in the aftermath of this deed, Baal managed to obtain for himself a palace (II AB; V AB). In Mesopotamia Marduk was gladly given a house by the divine fathers in recognition of his deeds on their behalf. In the Canaanite myth Baal's destruction of Yam-Nahar initially went unrecognized by his father. As it turns out father El had to be browbeaten into allowing his son to have a house of his own. The goddess Anath, Baal's sister, plays a particularly important role in this part of the drama. When she learns that her brother, in spite of his victory over Sea-River (Yam-Nahar), is still living at home and without a house of his own, she is furious and threatens to bloody her father's gray hair if he doesn't do something (V AB E, 6–14).

A kind of crescendo in the Baal stories is reached in a final episode where yet another member of this divine family is introduced, one whose destructive fury no one, apparently, not even Baal, can tame or control. This is El's son Mot (death) who, "one lip to earth and one to heaven" (I AB ii, 1), swallows him, thereby consigning him to the nether world. In the face of this tragedy father El is portrayed as particularly helpless and distraught. Earlier he was ready enough to let Baal be taken captive by Yam-Nahar. But now that Baal is actually dead, he descends from his throne, throws himself into the dust and covers his loins with sackcloth (I AB vi). Salvation comes not from him, but again from Baal's sister Anath who somehow rescues him from Mot's jaws.

Thus in Canaanite mythology as in Mesopotamia, it is not the father but the son (and in this instance also his sister) who creates the conditions necessary for a tolerable existence in this dangerous universe. And more often than not, they do this not with the father's blessing and help, but either in opposition to him, or in the face of his pathetic weakness. Fathers head up the cosmic home, these myths seem to be saying. They can even be kindly at times and emotionally involved in what is happening around them. But for the most part they are mere figureheads, not the ones really in charge.

OSIRIS AND ISIS

Basic clues to the dynamics at work in Egyptian life and religion can also be found in myths that functioned paradigmatically throughout Egyptian history. The most important of these, strangely enough, are nowhere to be found in their entirety in extant Egyptian literature. For their preservation we are indebted to the Greek historian Plutarch who lived in the first century A.D. and pieced them together from written and oral traditions available to him at that time.[8] They concern the Egyptian parental deities Isis (mother) and Osiris (father). The stories begin by telling of the benevolent rule of father Osiris over Egypt by means of which he was able to bring widespread peace and prosperity. He then set about carrying his teachings to the rest of the world. During his absence his sister-wife Isis ruled Egypt in his place.

A dark turning point in the story occurred, however, upon his return when a banquet was held in his honor to which his brother Set, along with others, had been invited. During the banquet a coffin was brought into the hall and Osiris was tricked into lying in it. When he did so, Set and those with him rose up and put a lid on the box, took it from the banquet hall and floated it down the Nile River. This might have been the end of the story, were it not for the reaction of Isis. Briefly summarized, she set off in search of her husband's corpse, eventually found it, brought it back to Egypt and conceived a son, Horus, by it. Once again, however, the wicked Set entered the picture. Having learned of the return of his brother's corpse, he stole it and, after chopping it into fourteen pieces, scattered them all over Europe. Isis, however, rescued her husband a second time and now by means of magical rites and incantations succeeded in restoring him to life in the afterworld. There, the Egyptians believed, Osiris continued to reign, his benevolent image, in the course of time, merging with that of the solar deity Re (sun). A final chapter of the myth relates how Osiris commissioned and empowered his son, Horus, to avenge his murder. This Horus subsequently did in several bloody battles in which Set was roundly defeated and destroyed.

Unique to this myth, in comparison to the Mesopotamian and Canaanite stories we have just reviewed, is the degree to which there is present here a powerful, wise father who brought peace to Egypt and in doing so succeeded as well in winning the loyalty and respect of wife and son. But here too the image of the father is a flawed one. How easily Osiris was outwitted by his wicked brother! He would appear to be naive. As a consequence his wife and son were compelled to play excessively demanding roles on his behalf. True, in Egyptian imagination Osiris was the ultimate power who ruled the universe from his home in eternity, but the stories declared that his very existence there was due to the salvific action of his wife, and it was his son finally who had to rule on earth and vindicate his name. In Egypt too, as in Mesopotamia and Canaan, a son, and in this instance also his mother, are the ultimate guarantors of the triumph of life over death.[9]

THE BIBLE

The Bible has no stories to tell about its god comparable to those we have just surveyed. And yet it would be misleading to say that it has no myths. Rather here there has occurred "a reorientation of the locale of myth," as John Priest has put it.[10] Instead of interacting with other gods the biblical God is portrayed in his relations with an historical people, Israel. Thus "the history of Israel is the biography" of its god and "the mode of the Israelite expression of myth."[11]

Three characteristics of the god so revealed are highlighted in almost all the stories about him. There is first of all the fact that he is "he" (and not "she").[12] This "he," of course, is a divine father (Dt 32:6; Jer 3:19; Is 63:16; Mal 2:10; Lk 11:2; Eph 3:14f), not a son, and one who in some sense is like the god of the fathers (Ex 3:15) and "El," the father of the gods (Gen 33:20; Jos 22:22).[13]

Contrasting sharply, however, with every other father deity we have looked at so far is his insistence, secondly, that those who serve him shall serve him exclusively and alone (Ex 20:3; Dt 5:7). This unique attribute is explained in several texts as resulting from his "jealousy" (Ex 20:5; Dt 5:9; 32:16; Jos 24:19; Num 25:11). In one text his very name is said to be "the jealous one" for, it adds, "a jealous god (el) is he" (Ex 34:14).[14] Being father (and not mother), this jealousy must be understood, first of all, as paternal jealousy directed against competing mother, son and daughter deities for the right to primacy in his own family. In other words, in biblical myth a divine father has divested himself, so to speak, of the cowardice and passivity so often attributed to fathers in extra-biblical myth and is viewed as taking charge of the affairs of his household (Ex 4:22b–23).

The very name of this god, Yahweh, may itself be symbolic of this remarkable transformation. It is quite likely a third person singular (masculine) causative form of the verb "to be" ("he causes to be") and there are reasons to think that originally it may have been used in conjunction with "el" (god), as in Psalm 10:12, with the meaning: "el causes to be."[15] To the question *what* god (or el) causes to be, Parke-Taylor has argued that it is his own people.[16] This in any case is the answer implied by Psalm 100, Isaiah 43:1

and Deuteronomy 32:6, the latter of which asks: "Is it not he (Yahweh) your father, who created you, who made you and established you?" Yahweh then is a divine father, but unlike his paternal contemporaries, a uniquely active one ("he causes to be"). In his zeal (jealousy) he created a people among whom he lives as the sole guiding force.

A third characteristic of this god is his goodness. This was unforgettably demonstrated by the very way he created a people in the first place: his liberating them from slavery (Ex 15) and his gracious covenant involving stipulations (Ex 20), all of which were seen to be for the well-being of the community (Ps 15:7–11). But this was also the essence of what was revealed concerning him in a remarkable audition that occurred in the aftermath of these events. To Moses' request for a glimpse of his "glory" (Ex 33:18), Yahweh passed before him and proclaimed, "Yahweh, Yahweh, a God (el) merciful and gracious, slow to anger, great in goodness and faithfulness . . ." (Ex 34:6f. *Jerusalem Bible*).[17]

This by and large (with now this, now that feature emphasized) is the portrait of God that we encounter throughout the biblical story, Old and New Testaments. There is one God and one God only to be worshiped and served. He is a divine father, yet not cowardly or withdrawn like so many of his paternal contemporaries, but alert rather, vigorously involved and uniformly just, kind and compassionate. "You, Yahweh, you yourself are our Father, our Redeemer is your ancient name" (Is 63:16b. *Jerusalem Bible*). "Our Father, who art in heaven, hallowed be thy name (Mt 6:9).

Only here in the myths of the ancient near east is it said that a father-god, worthy of being hallowed, is fully in charge of the cosmic home.

CONCLUDING COMMENTS

The main purpose of this essay, as previously stated, has been to highlight the contrasts that emerge when the divine father in biblical myth is compared with father divinities in several contemporary ancient near eastern mythologies. Such a comparison, as noted, raises questions about the assumption that biblical father religion is simply continuous with wider ancient near eastern patriarchalism. It would appear to be more accurate to say, as does David Bakan, that the Bible registers an important socioreligious shift, one in which, on the human level, men began assuming a larger role in the care of their families.[18] That men will do this, or do it well, history teaches, cannot be taken for granted. A "crisis of paternalization," as Bakan terms it, is not only associated with certain periods in history; it is one that is repeated in the individual life histories of many males who become fathers, generation after generation.[19] And in this may lie, in part at least, the relevance of the Bible right down to the present. Its firm belief in God as effectively caring father undergirds and encourages human fathers in the taking on of caretaking roles. In the light of what we now know about the importance of fathering for the emotional well-being of children, this may be viewed in itself as a not inconsiderable contribution to the life of the world.[20]

Notes

1. Joseph Campbell, *The Hero with a Thousand Faces*, Bollingen Series XVII (Princeton: Princeton University Press, 1949), p. 19.
2. Philip Slater, *The Glory of Hera: Greek Mythology and the Greek Family* (Boston: Beacon Press, 1968), p. xvi.
3. According to E. O. James, *The Worship of the Sky-God: A Comparative Study in Semitic and Indo-European Religion* (University of London: The Athlone Press, 1963), p. 8, father deities tend to be *Deus otiosus* and marginal to the cult "everywhere in primitive states of culture both in the present and the past."
4. My thesis is thus almost the opposite of the one put forward by Naomi Goldenberg in *Changing of the Gods: Feminism and the End of Traditional Religions* (Boston: Beacon Press, 1979), p. 37, who writes that "all recorded history has been patriarchal" and that for the first time today (in the wake of the feminist movement) we are about to see "what happens when

father-gods die for an entire culture. . . ." The truth is (as I will try to show) that father gods were far from alive and well even in antiquity (also see n. 3 above).

5. In the analysis that follows references are to the translation of this myth by E. A. Speiser in *Ancient Near Eastern Texts*, ed. by James Pritchard (Princeton: Princeton University Press, 1955), pp. 60–72.

6. For an analysis of this epic as a story about resistances to growing up, see Thorkild Jacobson, *The Treasures of Darkness: A History of Mesopotamian Religion* (New Haven: Yale University Press, 1976), pp. 218–219.

7. For convenience sake, references in the following discussion are to the widely accessible translation of these myths by H. L. Ginsberg in *Ancient Near Eastern Texts* (see n. 6 above) where an older numbering system is used than the one now in vogue; see J. C. L. Gibson, *Canaanite Myths and Legends* (Edinburgh: T. & T. Clark, 1977).

8. For an English translation of Plutarch's rendering of these myths see J. Griffiths, *Plutarch's De Iside et Osiride: Edited with an Introduction, Translation and Commentary* (University of Wales Press, 1970).

9. Concerning the way this myth reflected and influenced father-son-mother relations in Egyptian society see Jan Assmann, "Das Bild des Vaters im alten Agypten," in *Das Vaterbild in Mythos und Geschichte*, ed. by Bornkamm, et al. (Stuttgart: Kohlhammer, 1976), pp. 24–27.

10. John Priest, "Myth and Dream in Hebrew Scripture," in *Myths, Dreams and Religion*, ed. by Joseph Campbell (New York: E. P. Dutton and Co., 1970), p. 55.

11. *Ibid.*, p. 56.

12. The pronoun "he" is very close to being a divine name in the expression "I am he" (Dt 32:39; Is 43:10; etc.), "you are he" (Ps 102:27). On this usage and the possible importance of "he" as an initial focus of cultic devotion in biblical religion, see S. Mowinckel, "The Name of the God of Moses," *Hebrew Union College Annual*, 33 (1961), pp. 121–133.

13. El is both the name of the Canaanite father deity and the generic term for god. Evidence pointing to a link between

Canaanite El and the God of the Bible is reviewed by J. J. M. Roberts, "El," in *Interpreter's Dictionary of the Bible*, Supplementary Volume (Nashville: Abingdon, 1976), pp. 255–258. Concerning the representation of God as father in the Bible see Robert Hammerton-Kelly, *God the Father: Theology and Patriarchy in the Teaching of Jesus* (Philadelphia: Fortress Press, 1979).

14. The characterization of Yahweh as "jealous" is "the basic element in the whole OT idea of God," according to Walter Eichrodt, *Theology of the Old Testament*, vol. 1 (Philadelphia: Westminster Press, 1961), p. 210, n. 1.

15. The literature and arguments leading to this conclusion are reviewed by G. H. Parke-Taylor, *Yahweh: The Divine Name in the Bible* (Waterloo: Wilfrid Laurier Univ. Press, 1975), pp. 46–52.

16. *Ibid.*, pp. 60–61.

17. Concerning the central importance of this passage in Old Testament theology, see Brevard Childs, *The Book of Exodus: A Critical, Theological Commentary* (Philadelphia: Westminster, 1974), p. 615.

18. David Bakan, *And They Took Themselves Wives: The Emergence of Patriarchy in Western Civilization* (San Francisco: Harper & Row, 1979), p. 13.

19. *Ibid.*

20. Further to this point, see my, "The Contemporary Fathering Crisis: The Bible and Research Psychology," *The Conrad Grebel Review*, Fall 1983, pp. 21–37. (Chapter 8 in this volume.)

5

DEPATRIARCHALIZING GOD
IN BIBLICAL INTERPRETATION:
A CRITIQUE

The proposal that God is sometimes thought of as feminine or genderless in biblical tradition is not supported by the evidence. On the other hand, Yahweh is not simply regarded as male either, but as a father whose caring is often experienced as mother-like in its tenderness and compassion.

In an innovative essay entitled "Depatriarchalizing in Biblical Interpretation," published over a decade ago, Phyllis Trible sounded a theme that has become increasingly powerful in modern biblical study.[1] While biblical religion is clearly patriarchal, she wrote, not a few biblical texts point beyond patriarchy to a more egalitarian ideal in human relations.[2] Indeed, she argued, a "depatriarchalizing principle" is at work in scripture which, once recognized, permits us "to translate biblical faith without sexism" on the authority of the biblical tradition itself.[3]

In this essay I will be focusing exclusively on the way Trible and others, in following through on this project, go about "depatriarchalizing" the biblical representation of *God*. Their point of view in summary is this:

(1) Biblical references to God as patriarch or father are sexist, in that maleness is thereby divinized and men are

encouraged to think of themselves as god-like in ways women cannot.

(2) Yet as a matter of fact a patriarchal or masculine representation of God is not nearly as predominant in the Bible as generally thought. Indeed there are biblical texts that either deny that God is male, or portray him as female, or as above and beyond gender altogether.

(3) Consequently, biblical tradition itself can be said to temper and relativize the sexist patriarchal notion of God to be found there in many passages.

So far as I know these novel ideas, which are already enshrined in Trible's essay on "God" in the *IDBS*,[4] have to date not been seriously questioned. And yet, as I hope to indicate, the evidence cited thus far in their support is far from cogent.

In the critique that follows I will be focusing for the most part on the second of the two points referred to above: that there are texts in the Bible that either deny that God is male or portray him as female or as above and beyond gender altogether. But to avoid misunderstanding as to what my motives are in making this critique, I will begin with a few comments regarding the first and third points as well: that the biblical representation of God as father is a sexist notion that needs to be tempered and relativized.

IS THE REPRESENTATION OF GOD AS FATHER, AS SUCH, A SEXIST NOTION?

There appears to be an unexamined assumption in the writings of Trible and others that "patriarchy" has to do quite simply with male supremacy and that this is demeaning for women. If God is male, the argument goes, then male is God and it follows that whenever God is represented as male-patriarch, females are prejudicially denigrated and males favored.[5] But is this analysis adequate?

As some indication that it is not, it should be noted that the term "patriarch" refers not to males as such, but to a quite specific male role: that of "pater" or father. Moreover, the "supremacy" of males in this role (if such it is) is one that has an impact for good or ill not only on females, but on males also, for men as fathers, together with their wives, exercise responsibility for the care of children of both sexes. This suggests that for an appreciation of "pater" as divine metaphor we must attend to the dynamics of fathering in the nurture of children and not just to the issue of male supremacy as it affects women.

Those who have done this stress that for an adequate understanding of the significance of the father-role some awareness is needed, first of all, of the strength of the bond that typically exists between *mothers* and children by virtue of their symbiotic tie during pregnancy, birth and nursing.[6] It is this biologically determined relationship, so essential in laying the foundations of healthy development, that shapes those qualities usually associated with mothering: unconditional availability, receptivity and tenderness. Fathers, on the other hand, when effectively present to their families, insert themselves into the bond between mother and child as a "second other" by an initiative very much like that of adoption. Where this initiative is energetic and winsome, developmental psychology teaches us, an essential autonomy from the mother is fostered and children of both sexes are significantly helped in orienting themselves to the cultural universe outside the home with its laws and ethical norms. Maternal values are not thereby repudiated—fathers too may embody tender mother-like attributes without ceasing to be fathers—but the exclusivity of the mother-bond is challenged by an authority that separates the child and orients it toward its personal future in extra-familial society.[7]

Seen in this light the metaphor "father," when used of God, is far from being simply a symbol of masculine dominance or privilege. It may in fact embrace feminine or maternal attributes, but in combination with what Vergote terms "firmness and directive action."[8] "If the father symbolizes God better than the mother," he adds, "it is thus because of that which paternal law effects in the family triangle."[9]

In arguing then, as I will in the following section, that the biblical representation of God is more, not less patriarchal than generally recognized, and that the texts cited to the contrary do not say what they are said to be saying by Trible and others, I trust I will not be misunderstood as favoring the denigration of women. On the contrary there are solid reasons for thinking that the biblical representation of God as caring father has had a generally humanizing effect in the lives of both men and women.[10]

DOES THE BIBLE ITSELF DEPATRIARCHALIZE GOD?

The data that Trible and others appeal to as evidence of depatriarchalizing God in the Bible may be classified in a three-fold manner:

(1) texts ascribing feminine activities or emotions to God;
(2) terms used to characterize God whose root meanings are feminine;
(3) texts explicitly stating that God is not male, hence intimating that God is beyond gender altogether.

This third group of texts, I suggest, merits our attention first of all, for were it true, as Trible has put it, that they intimate that "Israel was quite aware that a masculine label for Deity is dangerous"[11] and that hence "all analogies to the freedom and transcendence of God are inadequate,"[12] then this might have implications for the way the additional evidence for depatriarchalizing God referred to above is to be understood.

But are there in fact biblical texts that point to a God beyond gender?

It may be noted to begin with that the passages cited in support of this thesis are very few in number—three to be exact: Numbers 23:19; 1 Samuel 15:29; Hosea 11:9. Considering the size of the biblical canon, this in itself is remarkable. Here and nowhere else is there even an inkling of such an idea. Furthermore, a comparison of the three texts quickly indicates that two of them, Numbers 23:19 and 1 Samuel 15:29, are virtually identical, and the third, Hosea 11:9, is quite similar to the other two.

But do even these three texts say what Trible suggests they say? Both Numbers 23:19 and 1 Samuel 15:29 declare that "God is not man ('*îš*)" in the specific sense that he does not lie. The contrast then is *not* between a God beyond gender and "man" as male. In fact such a contrast is excluded by the second line in both texts which states that neither is God "*ādām*" (1 Sam 15:29) or "*ben 'ādām*" (Num 23:19) "that he should repent." "*'Ādām*" is the Hebrew term for "human being" inclusive of both sexes (Gen 1:31). Hosea 11:9 differs from the other two texts only in the sense that there God himself says: "For I am God and not '*îš*," and specifies as the point of contrast, not that he does not lie, but that he ("the holy one in your midst") is full of compassion.

These texts then are quite specific as to the point of the contrast between God and man and quite deliberate in clarifying that by "*'îš*" is meant not "male" but "*'ādām*" (human being). Furthermore, in all three texts "God" is referred to as "*'ēl*," a general term for deity, but also the name of the Canaanite father deity. In Numbers 23:19 it is said of this "*'ēl*": "has *he* spoken and shall *he* not do it, has *he* uttered his word and shall *he* not make good?" In short, the deity referred to here is clearly identified as masculine-paternal. How then can it be argued on the basis of these texts that a "masculine label" for deity was thought to be dangerous or that a depatriarchalizing principle was at work in biblical religion?

But if it is misleading to suggest that biblical authors ever thought of God as above or beyond gender, are there not certain texts that "temper" the dominance of the masculine-patriarchal image of God there by suggesting that he could, on occasion at least, be thought of as female or mother?

As noted, two types of evidence have been put forward in defense of this thesis:

- texts, first of all, which purportedly ascribe feminine characteristics or emotions to God;
- terms characterizing God whose root meanings are feminine.

In this latter category are two terms in particular: the Hebrew adjective "*raḥûm*" (meaning "compassion"), which Trible points out is based on the Hebrew root "*reḥem*" (meaning "womb"), and "*Šadday*" which Trible, following Cross, believes originally meant "breasts."[13] "Used only of deity," Trible writes, "*raḥûm* is not language for a father who creates by begetting but for a mother who creates by nourishing in the womb."[14] Bearing this in mind Trible translates the verb "*rāḥam*" as "mother compassion" in Jeremiah 31:20 where God is quoted as saying of Ephraim: "For as often as I speak of him, I do remember him still. Therefore my inner parts yearn for him; I will surely have mother compassion on him. . . ."[15]

Were this translation correct, why would it be inappropriate for Yahweh as father to say that he yearns for his children with motherly compassion? Cannot fathers also experience "motherly compassion"? As a matter of fact "*raḥûm*" occurs frequently in Canaanite texts as a characterization of the Canaanite father deity "*Ēl*," and in Psalm 103:13, as Trible herself has noted,[16] it is said quite explicitly that "as a father pities [or has compassion for] his children, so Yahweh pities [or has compassion for] those who fear him."[17]

Clearly, then, in the ancient near east at least, fathers, human and divine, were readily characterized as having compassion. Needless to say, root meanings of words do not necessarily determine subsequent usages, a point that applies as well to Trible's suggestion that in Genesis 49:25 "the God of thy father" is balanced by a maternal image implicit in the name *Šadday*, because of its possible root meaning "breasts" and the occurrence of the word "breasts" (*šādaym*) at the verse's end. Even were this etymology correct (a derivation from a root word meaning "field" has also been defended),[18] its secondary meaning, Cross notes, was evidently "mountain,"[19] the abode of "*Ēl*" in Canaanite mythology. It is once again difficult to see how an argument for the existence of a depatriarchalizing principle in biblical tradition can be made on such a basis.

We are left then, as evidence of depatriarchalizing tendencies in the Bible, with those passages where it is intimated that God acts in maternal or feminine ways or has feminine qualities or emotions. Examples would be: Genesis 1:26–27, where both male and female are said to have been created in the image and likeness of God; Psalm 22:9–10, where Yahweh is likened to a midwife; Deuteronomy 32:18, where he is referred to as "the God who gave you birth"; Numbers 11:12, where Moses asks

"Have I given birth to this people?"—alluding, it is suggested, to the fact that it is God who like a mother really gave birth to Israel; Isaiah 42:14a, where God calls out like a woman in travail; Isaiah 49:15, where God says that even if a mother forgets her baby at the breast, "I will not forget" (thus likening himself to a mother); Isaiah 66:9, where God is characterized as the one who brings to birth and comforts Jerusalem as a mother comforts a child; Psalm 131:2, where the psalmist declares that his soul is quieted before God, like a child quieted at its mother's breast (implying thereby that God is like a mother to him).

There can be no doubt that these and several other texts that might perhaps be added to this list[20] do attribute mother-like or feminine actions and attributes to God. The point at issue is whether in doing so God is actually thought of *as* mother (and not just mother-*like*). This is excluded by the fact that the texts in question clearly and consistently maintain a paternal-masculine point of reference. Not once in the Bible is God addressed as mother, said to be mother, or referred to with feminine pronouns. On the contrary, gender usage throughout clearly specifies that the root metaphor is masculine-father.

Psalm 22:9–10 is a case in point. Concerning this text Trible has written: "Deity" is here portrayed as "both midwife and mother. She [sic] takes the infant from the womb and places it safely upon maternal breasts; in turn she becomes the very one upon whom the child is cast from birth."[21] But the text itself nowhere refers to God as "she." Psalm 22:9 is a prayer which opens and closes with an invocative "you" which in Hebrew has a masculine form (*'attâ*) and a feminine form (*'att*). In his prayer the psalmist uses the *masculine* "you" (*'attâ*), as one would expect of a worshiper addressing Yahweh: "Yes you [masculine]," he prays, "drew me out of the womb, entrusted me to my mother's breasts; cast upon you from the womb, from my mother's belly you [masculine] have been my God."

It is clearly not true then that the psalmist in this passage is actually thinking of Yahweh *as* midwife or mother. Rather *like* a gentle midwife, he says, you, Yahweh, have been my guardian from the moment of my birth. Here as throughout the Hebrew Bible Yahweh is portrayed as a caring, resourceful father. Genesis

1:26–27 (cited by Trible as a "topical clue" in her most ambitious work on this subject)[22] is no exception. After declaring "Let us make man (*'ādām*) in our image . . ." the text specifies, "So God created man [male and female] in *his* image . . ." (Gen 1:27). Apparently biblical authors saw no incongruity in characterizing both men and women as bearing the image and likeness of a paternal deity.

SUMMARY AND CONCLUSIONS

In her initial essay calling for depatriarchalizing in biblical interpretation Trible concluded that modern assertions that God is masculine, even when they are qualified, are misleading and detrimental if not altogether inaccurate, for "unlike fertility gods, Yahweh is neither male nor female; neither he nor she."[23] In this essay I too have tried to indicate that referring to Yahweh simply as male is to misconstrue the issues. Already at its point of origins biblical Yahwism sought to differentiate itself not only from the worship of feminine deities but alternative masculine deities as well (Baal, for example, the Canaanite son-deity). On the other hand it had no hesitation confessing that a continuity existed between Yahweh and the Canaanite father deity El ("El of gods is Yahweh"—Jos 22:22).[24]

Yahweh then is not simply male, but father to his worshipers[25] as the name Yahweh itself may imply ("he causes to be").[26] True, Yahweh as father is pictured occasionally as acting with a tenderness and care that is mother-like. But nowhere is it ever said or suggested that he *is* mother. According to Jesus his very "name" is father and the hallowing of that name is the focal point of religious devotion.[27] "The God of Judaism is undoubtedly a father-symbol and father image," Raphael Patai has written, "possibly the greatest such symbol and image conceived by man. Nor," he adds, "can there be any doubt as to the psychological need answered by this image. This, together with the great moral imperatives, was the unique contribution of prophetic Judaism to mankind."[28]

Notes

1. Phyllis Trible, "Depatriarchalizing in Biblical Interpretation," *JAAR* 41 (1973), pp. 30–48. For a review of feminist research on God symbolism, including that of Trible, see Carol Christ, "Symbols of Goddess and God in Feminist Theology," in Carl Olsen, ed., *The Book of the Goddess Past and Present: An Introduction to Her Religion* (New York: Crossroad, 1983), pp. 231–251.
2. Trible, "Depatriarchalizing," p. 31.
3. *Ibid.*, pp. 31, 48.
4. Phyllis Trible, "God, Nature of, in the OT," *IDBS* (Nashville: Abingdon Press, 1976), pp. 368–369.
5. For a sophisticated critique of biblical patriarchy based on this assumption, see Sallie McFague, *Metaphorical Theology: Models of God in Religious Language* (Philadelphia: Fortress, 1982), pp. 145–177.
6. The analysis here is that of religious psychologist Antoine Vergote. See especially his essays, "The Parental Figures: Symbolic Functions and Medium for the Representation of God," and "Overview and Theoretical Perspective," chs. 1 and 8, in *The Parental Figures and the Representation of God: A Psychological and Cross-Cultural Study*, eds. Antoine Vergote and Alvero Tamayo (The Hague/Paris/New York: Mouton, 1981) 13, pp. 186, 220.
7. *Ibid.*, pp. 195–196. See also Vergote's discussion of these issues in his *The Religious Man: A Psychological Study of Religious Attitudes* (Dublin: Gill and Macmillan, 1969), pp. 143–200. For an excellent summary of the current research on fathering see the thirty-six essays in *Father and Child: Developmental and Clinical Perspectives*, eds. Stanley Cath, et al. (Boston: Little, Brown, 1982).
8. *The Religious Man*, p. 177.
9. Vergote, *Parental Figures*, p. 220.
10. Further to this point see my "The Contemporary Fathering Crisis: The Bible and Research Psychology," *Conrad Grebel Review* 1 (Fall 1983), pp. 22–37 (Chapter 8 in this volume). Concerning the relatively "high status" of women in the Old

Testament, see John H. Otwell, *And Sarah Laughed: The Status of Women in the Old Testament* (Philadelphia: Westminster, 1977); Hans Walter Wolff, *Anthropology of the Old Testament* (Philadelphia: Fortress, 1974), pp. 169–173.

11. "Depatriarchalizing," p. 32.

12. "God, Nature of, in the OT," p. 369.

13. *Ibid.*, p. 368.

14. *Ibid.*

15. *Ibid.*

16. *Ibid.*

17. On "*ēl raḥûm*" (Ex 34:6; Ps 86:15) as one example among many of Yahweh's "debt to El's Canaanite past," see J.J.M. Roberts, "El," *IDBS*, p. 257.

18. For an analysis of the complex issues involved in establishing the etymology of this word see Frank Moore Cross, *Canaanite Myth and Hebrew Epic: Essays in the History of the Religion of Israel* (Cambridge: Harvard University, 1973), pp. 52–56.

19. *Ibid.*, p. 55.

20. For several additional suggestions see Virginia Ramey Mollenkott, *The Divine Feminine: The Biblical Imagery of God as Female* (New York: Crossroad, 1983).

21. Trible, "God, Nature of, in the OT," p. 368.

22. *God and the Rhetoric of Sexuality*, Overtures to Biblical Theology, eds. Walter Brueggemann, John Donahue (Philadelphia: Fortress, 1978), pp. 12–23.

23. Trible, "Depatriarchalizing," p. 34.

24. On this point, see again J. J. M. Roberts, "El," pp. 255–258.

25. God is referred to as father twenty-one times in the Old Testament, two hundred and fifty-five times in the New Testament, according to Felix Donahue, "The Spiritual Father in the Scriptures," in *Abba: Guides to Wholeness and Holiness East and West*, ed. John R. Sommerfeldt (Kalamazoo: Cistercian, 1982), pp. 3, 6. Malachi is thus only stating the obvious when he asks: "Have we not all one father? Has not one God created us?" (Mal 2:10).

26. The literature and arguments leading to this conclusion are reviewed by G. H. Parke-Taylor, *Yahweh: The Divine Name in*

the Bible (Waterloo: Wilfrid Laurier University, 1975), pp. 46–52.

27. Lk 11:2; Jn 17:6, 11, 12, 26.
28. Raphael Patai, *The Hebrew Goddess* (New York: Avon Books, 1967), p. 9.

PART THREE
HUMAN FATHERING IN BIBLICAL TRADITION

> When I was a son with my father,
> tender, the only one in the sight
> of my mother,
> he taught me. . . .*

* Prv 4:3f.

6

NEW MODES OF HUMAN FATHERING (HEBREW BIBLE)

Through the rituals of redemption of the first-born, circumcision, and passover faith in God as redemptive, caring father was linked to human fathering and Israelite fathers came to be involved in the care and teaching of their own children to a degree that was unique in the world of their time.

In this essay I want to indicate how in connection with the revelation of God as father in biblical tradition there emerged in Israel a new appreciation for the role and function of a certain kind of human fathering, and how new modes of fathering actually did come into existence there in this context. I want to be careful not to overstate my case in this regard. I am not referring to a sudden, radical change whereby Israelite fathers became ideal fathers. I do not know, if we had the means for measuring this, whether overall during the centuries when the Hebrew Bible was coming into existence, Israelite fathers would stand out as all that different from their counterparts in other cultures. What I am suggesting is that under the influence of their experience of God as caring, redemptive father (Is 63:16), especially from the days of Moses and Israel's exodus from Egypt onward (Dt 32:6), innovations in fathering were introduced that over the centuries did serve to consolidate and strengthen the role of men as fathers in their families to a degree unknown elsewhere in the ancient world.[1]

The chief heir and custodian of these biblical innovations in fathering in the modern world are the Jews, since Christians, even though regarding Hebrew scripture as part of their scriptures too, have by and large ignored those texts that prescribe for the new modes of fathering I am going to be discussing. In fact, it might be said that a critical distinction between Judaism and Christianity arises right at this point. Whereas Judaism has both continued and elaborated the father-family traditions enshrined in Hebrew scripture, Christianity has to some considerable extent relaxed or ignored these traditions. I will be saying more about *this* issue elsewhere (see Chapters 7 and 10). Here, I will be concentrating on identifying and explaining the innovations themselves.

There are two types of data especially I will be looking at in this regard. There are, to begin with, certain *rituals* or liturgies that merit careful study—rites in which fathers play the leading roles, and which, I hope to show, reveal certain new trends in fathering. And then I will be looking at evidence that points to the emergence of a unique sense of responsibility among Israelite fathers for being the *teachers* of their children.

There is a third set of data bearing on fathering in Israel the importance of which needs to be recognized and acknowledged, even though I will not be discussing it in any detail. I refer to the way biblical tradition upholds the integrity of the marital bond between a man and his wife by its very explicit and detailed teaching against adultery in all of its forms—whether as incest (see Lev 18; 20:8–21), or philandering (see Prv 5; 7:6–27), or as the outright seduction of another man's wife (Ex 20:14). Needless to say, where adultery is *not* proscribed in this outright manner, the foundations of the father-involved family are undermined. Israel was therefore not unjustified in regarding its teachings and laws on this issue specifically as among its most important distinguishing characteristics. Failure to hold firm on this point, it was believed, would result in her being "vomited out" of the land (Lev 18:24, 28). Marital fidelity, on the other hand, guaranteed the stability of the two-parent family and helped to secure the respect due to both parents, father and mother.[2]

FATHER-FAMILY RITUALS

Too little attention has been paid in the study of the Hebrew Bible, by Christians especially, to the rituals prescribed there. It is these, very often, that are the keys to an understanding of the structures of faith that were predominant. As "little dramas" repeatedly enacted, rituals embody and communicate to successive generations the world outlook of those who perform them—what they believe to be important.

When we do take note of this point, one soon becomes aware of the striking fact that among the most important biblical rituals are several having to do with the family, and with the *father's* role in the family in particular. It can then also be readily observed that the editors of the Bible have preserved the records of these particular rituals in Exodus 12 and 13, right in the midst of their narrative accounts of Israel's foundational experience of exodus and liberation from Egypt. Obviously, their purpose in doing so was to communicate their conviction that it would be precisely by means of the enactment of these rituals in particular that the memory and significance of Israel's experience with God at this foundational juncture of its existence could best be kept alive.

The actions or rituals alluded to in these chapters are three-fold:

- passover (here combined with the festival of unleavened bread—12:1–28; 13:3–10);
- redemption of the first-born (12:43–51; 13:1–2; 13:11–16);
- circumcision—this latter being more presupposed than commanded in the instructions of this section (12:48–51).

THE RITUALS AS A GROUP

Before examining these rituals individually and trying to ascertain their significance, I would like to try to characterize them as a group. And the first thing I want to emphasize is that each of them is in fact a ritual, a little drama, a *sacred* drama, and that such dramas are hereby given a central place in the life of the biblical community. Biblical faith is not so much taught as caught, not so much transmitted (from generation to generation) through formal teaching as by means of symbolic actions.

But just as noteworthy is the fact, secondly, that these rituals are rites of the *family* (as just suggested)—and of the *nuclear* family specifically—not rites of the sanctuary or of the community as a whole. In other words, these oldest and most enduring religious ceremonies are *nuclear family* affairs (that is, actions of the household of father, mother, children, servants and guests resident in, or attached to, this primary unit).

Furthermore, and equally important, I suggest (and this point too is not usually sufficiently noted or emphasized), they are family rituals in which the *father* plays the leading role.

Finally, all of these father-family rituals have to do with the father's role as caretaker and guardian of his *children* above all. Hence, they may be characterized as father-family rituals in which the father is called upon to perform or do certain actions bearing upon the well-being of his progeny.

Let us look now more closely at each of these rituals in this light.

REDEMPTION OF THE FIRST-BORN

I will begin our survey with what might well have been the oldest of these ritual actions: the redemption of the first-born. In the background is the widespread practice of ritually slaughtering a first-born as an act of piety and devotion to God (as dramatized in the near slaughter of Isaac by his father Abraham in Genesis 22). The shape of the exodus narrative as a whole seems to reflect the background presence of this gruesome ritual.[3] In the story of the plagues, for example, emphasis is placed on the fact that the tenth and most devasting of these, the one that set the stage for Israel's liberation from Egypt, was the slaughter of the *Egyptian* male first-born (Ex 12:21–34). This theme surfaces again in Exodus 13:1 in the commandment that *all* first-born, "the first birth from every womb . . . whether man or beast . . ." shall be consecrated to Yahweh (compare Ex 22:28–29), and then again in the ritual alluded to in 13:11–16, the one that declares that an exception shall be made in the case of first-born sons. They, it is specified, shall be "redeemed" by offering in their stead an animal sacrifice (13:13).

Given this cultural background the ritual of "the redemption of the first-born" must have been experienced as a most impressive one regarding which a first-born son, upon growing up, might indeed have remarked to his father (as it says he would, in Exodus 13:14), "What does this mean?"—to which the father was instructed to reply that this is a "sign on your hand" by which the memory will be kept alive that "Yahweh brought us out of Egypt with a mighty hand" (13:16).

In other words, through this ritual the hard-won insight (already embodied in the story of Abraham's near sacrifice of *his* first-born),[4] that God wants our devotion *not* that we kill our sons, was brought to dramatic, confessional expression—here, however, within the framework of the story of Israel's liberation from Egypt. Just as the tragic *death* of *Egypt's* first-born was ritually alluded to in the offering up of the first-born of the flocks, so the memory of the redemptive preservation of *Israel's* first-born during this same sequence of events was kept alive by the rite of the son's release. In this way the truth was dramatized that Israel's God is a "redemptive father" (Is 63:16) whom Israelite fathers should emulate in their care of the children given to them.

The spiritual dynamic embodied in this ritual can be sensed in the way it is still being enacted among Jews right down to the present.[5] As currently practiced, the redemption of a first-born son occurs on the child's thirty-first day of life, when it is more or less certain that the child will live. He is then brought by his father (in the presence of invited guests) to the rabbi in charge of a given synagogue. Instead of an animal sacrifice as substitute for the son, a coin, minted specifically for this ritual, is brought as the redemption offering.

As the father approaches the rabbi with his child, he is asked whether he wishes to redeem his child or leave him at the altar! The father in reply expresses his desire to redeem and keep his son, hands over the redemption money as a substitute, and then recites two benedictions: one for the fulfillment of the commandment of redemption and another a prayer of thanks. The rabbi then solemnly pronounces three times: "Your son is redeemed, your son is redeemed, your son is redeemed," after which he returns the child to his father.

The emotional impact that a ritual of this kind might have had (and has) on a father is only too obvious. Through it he is compelled to face up to the prospect of getting rid of his son, and he must make explicit and public his decision to redeem and keep him instead. He thereby pledges himself in the sight of God and his community to take ownership of this child—to keep and care for him—and gives voice to his gratitude for the privilege of being able to do so.

The son on his part grows to maturity knowing that he was redeemed by his father in this manner—knowing that he was wanted, chosen and loved by his father as an infant in a very deliberate, self-conscious way. This act, linked as it is to Yahweh's redemption of Israel, was simultaneously an expression of religious faith and commitment. To redeem and care for children in this manner was spiritually motivated; since this was what Yahweh himself had done in redeeming *his* children from Egypt, this is only what human fathers can be expected to do with their children as well.

The way this ritual has served through the centuries to consolidate paternal identities and cement the bonds between fathers and children in the community of those who practiced it should be evident.

CIRCUMCISION

But there was yet another father-ritual that made an even more important contribution to this same end, and this is the rite of circumcision. Its importance lies in part in the fact that this particular ritual was (and is) performed not just once in the life of a family, at the birth of a first-born son, but repeatedly in conjunction with the birth of every male child. Furthermore, the ritual action called for is more traumatic in some respects than the one enacted during the redemption of the first-born, for in this instance the father must wound his son in a manner that is painful and leaves a permanent mark on his body.

Circumcision refers to the removal of the foreskin of the

male penis. The resulting wound, of course, generally speaking, is a minor one, leaving the individual involved none the worse for it. As such it may be described as a "symbolic wound," for its significance lies not in the surgery itself so much as in what the surgery symbolizes—in the thoughts and emotions surrounding this action.

What were those? Since the biblical texts describing this ritual are rather vague on this point, it may be useful to look, first of all, at the meaning this ritual has had (and still has) in other cultural settings.[6] Among most extra-biblical peoples (the contemporary Muslim Arabs would be an example) circumcision functions as a *puberty* ritual marking the transition of young boys to adulthood. Felix Bryk, after a thorough review of the subject, sides with those who view it as having originated in the belief (possibly correct) that it increases male procreative power.[7] Thus, in most extra-biblical cultures it was (and is) regarded as a mark of manhood which is to be inscribed on the flesh *at puberty* preparatory to marriage. In Israel too this close association of circumcision with puberty and marriage is preserved in the Hebrew terms for "bridegroom," "son-in-law" and "father-in-law," all of which are derived from the single Hebrew root which even today yet, in Arabic, means "to circumcise."[8]

However, viewed against this background, what is striking about the biblical circumcision ritual is the fact that here it was *not* performed at *puberty* (although there are passing references to this form of the ritual in the brief notice in Genesis 17:23 that Abraham circumcised his son Ishmael *when he was thirteen*). Nor was it carried out as a ritual of the community (although again there are hints of this custom as well; see Jos 5:2–9; Gen 34:13–19). Within biblical tradition another mode of celebration came into vogue (we are not sure just when this happened)—the one specified in two texts: Genesis 17:12 and Leviticus 12:3. These state that *each individual father* (rather than the fathers as a group) is to enact this ritual with his own sons, and to do so, not at puberty, but when his son is still a newborn infant, on the eighth day of his life. In Israel, in other words, circumcision was transformed into an infancy ritual—it was something a father did for his own male children while they were still infants.

Can we assume that in this form it had a meaning similar or identical with that which it had (and has) as a puberty ritual? The association of this infant circumsion ceremony in Genesis 17 with God's promise to Abraham to give him a great progeny would suggest as much. Among the Israelites too, in other words, procreativity and circumcision were intimately linked. This connection is also drawn in contemporary Jewish circumcision liturgies whose origins can be traced back into the first centuries of this era. According to Shoshana Matzner-Bekerman,[9] these begin with the mother bringing the child to the place where the ritual is to be performed. The child is then taken from her arms by an honored male guest, carried to another room where other male guests are assembled, and delivered to the father for the circumcision ritual proper.

At this point certain words are spoken that make quite explicit what its meaning is for the adults gathered. For example, at the opening of the ceremony the father prays, "Blessed be Thou, O Lord our God, King of the Universe, who has sanctified us by Thy commandments, and hast bidden us to make him enter into the covenant of Abraham our father." Those assembled reply: "As he has been entered into the covenant, so may he be introduced to the study of the Torah, to the marriage canopy, and to good deeds."

This particular prayer is repeated twice again during the remaining ceremony. Especially striking and surprising is the reference here to the "marriage canopy." In and through the circumcision ceremony the father declares his readiness to care for and nurture this infant son to the end that he will study Torah, eventually marry, and do good deeds. Thus, even though an *infancy* ritual, circumcision is performed with reference to that moment in life when this child will be a young adult, leave home and marry. It may thus be characterized as a puberty rite performed upon infants.

In other words, the biblical father does not wait until his son is an adolescent to prepare him for the decisive transition into adulthood, marriage, and a family of his own. He pledges himself to be involved to this end almost from the day of his son's birth.

Circumcision is the mark of this paternal covenant between father and son.

PASSOVER

There was a third family ritual introduced into the Israelite family system early on, one which, in some respects, would eventually have an even more significant impact on the Israelite father-involved family than either of those we have discussed to this point—and that was the passover celebration. Whereas redemption of the first-born was a ritual of the father carried out once in a lifetime (and only in connection with the eldest male child), and whereas circumcision was also a once-in-a-lifetime ritual for the specific male involved, the passover ceremonies recurred annually and culminated in a festive family meal in which the entire family (wives, sons, daughters, and family servants) participated. These facts alone begin to suggest some of the reasons why this particular ritual has played the tremendously significant role it has in Jewish family formation and survival right down to the present.

What is stressed in the liturgical instructions for the performance of this ritual in Exodus 12 and 13 are certain actions by the fathers of the community prior to the meal itself. First, four days before passover evening, a sheep or goat one year old is to be selected from the flock—one that is male and without blemish. Then, during the afternoon immediately prior to the passover, the community of male fathers is to gather and collectively kill the animals they have selected, and roast them. However, in addition to this, blood from the slain animals is to be taken and smeared on the doorposts and lintel of each of the houses where the passover lamb is going to be eaten. That same evening, then, after sundown, household by household, the roasted animals are to be eaten with unleavend bread and bitter herbs, within the confines and safety of the individual homes.

The texts describing this ritual go on to ascribe two meanings to this set of ritual actions, meanings that were to imprint themselves on the minds and hearts of its participants: (1) first of all, and in general, this meal was to be carried out as an act of remembrance of the time when God liberated his people Israel from Egypt; (2) but the meal was also meant to recall a quite specific feature of that liberation: those events related to the death of the Egyptian first-born and the sparing of the Israelite first-born. The texts recall that on the night of liberation a "destroyer" (as it is referred to in Exodus 12:23) ravaged the Egyptian households, killing all of their first-born sons, but·this "destroyer" *passed over* the Israelites. In Exodus 12:21–28 this destroyer is pictured as a destructive force that would kill anyone who, on this particular night, left his house and went outside. Hence the urgent command: "Let none of you venture out of the house until morning" (Ex 12:22). The blood of the slain passover lamb smeared by the father on the lintel of his house was regarded as a sign given by God as protection against this lethal danger.

It has been conjectured that passover was initially an ancient rite of shepherds, enacted just prior to their going with their flocks to summer pasturage as protection against the nameless demons that might assail them as they traveled. If so, among the Israelites this rite was appropriated as a ritual of the family under the leadership of the father in memory of Israel's origins as a people through Yahweh's saving them from destruction during their escape from Egypt. Just as Yahweh acted for salvation, so does the father. He too must save his family from the destructive forces that threaten it. While Yahweh is the ultimate redeemer, the fathers must act too (if their families are not to perish) by gathering their families around them within the intimacy of the four walls of their respective houses.

No other ritual drama portrays as forcefully as does this one the interplay between God as father and the Israelite father in the care of his children. It is the culmination and embodiment of the other two rituals. If redemption of the first-born and circumcision are adoption rituals initiating the father into his role as custodian and guide of his sons in particular, passover consolidates and expands that role, year after year, and makes it visible and accessible to the whole family. Through it fathers in Israel, as in no other culture we know of, appropriated to themselves an identity as redemptive caretakers, with an ongoing and permanent stake in the life of their families.

THE TEACHING FATHER

From this there emerged in Israel yet another role for fathers of great importance for the future of Israel and the faith it represented: that of the teaching father. This is the second development in fathering I want to discuss briefly. A good approach to this subject, I have found, is to look first at what is known about educational practices elsewhere in the ancient world of this period. This can provide us with a backdrop for identifying what is similar or distinctive about developments within biblical culture.

A valuable resource for such a study is William Barclay's beautifully written book entitled *Train Up a Child: Educational Ideals in the Ancient World.*[10] From reading what he has written there, one is impressed, first of all, at how diverse were the educational ideals and practices of the peoples of this period and region (first millennium B.C.). Each culture, it seems, and in some instances different regions within a culture, had differing ideas regarding how children should be taught, what they should be taught, and who should teach them.

In ancient Sparta, for example, the focus of education was on preparing children to participate in or support a *military* elite. Everything was geared to that end. Those unfit for this goal were identified at infancy and killed. Even the fit, however, were not permitted to remain with their mothers, but were given to the care of nurses especially skilled in diet and discipline. At about seven years of age children would begin attending state-run schools for training in the martial arts exclusively.

In Athens on the other hand a very different set of goals and methods was operative. There the raising up of a male *cultural* elite was the goal; slaves did all the mundane jobs of the society. Free-born males were thus free to devote virtually their entire lives to music, aesthetics, philosophy, athletics and the like. Women, for the most part, were excluded from these activities and confined to their homes and to caring for young children.

Ideally, as the Greeks viewed it, the home was to be the first schoolroom, but in point of fact the family life of the ancient Greeks was so unstable, and women so ignorant, that little education took place there. Private schools for boys (from six to eighteen), where reading, writing, simple arithmetic, poetry, music and graduated physical exercises were taught, were the bastion of Greek education.

Roman educational ideals and methods were somewhat different from either of these examples. At least initially (prior to the third century B.C.) ethical and social values were stressed and the expectation was that a Roman father would be much involved in the education of his own children. Indeed, some of the more inspiring passages quoted by Barclay from Roman sources are portraits of fathers who tried to hold on to this older educational ideal at a point when it was dying out. An example is Plutarch's description of a certain first century Roman senator named Cato, who once declared that:

> a man who struck his wife or his child was laying hands on the most holy of sacred things; that it was a greater honour to be a good husband than a distinguished senator, and that nothing was more admirable in old Socrates than that he lived in peace and quiet with a difficult wife and half-witted children. When Cato's son was born [Plutarch continued] no duty (save perhaps some public function) was so pressing as to prevent him from being present when his wife bathed the child and wrapped it in its swaddling clothes. . . . As soon as the boy was able to learn, Cato took him personally in charge and taught him his letters, even though he owned an accomplished slave who gave lessons to many boys. But Cato, to use his own words, would not have the slave abuse his son, nor perhaps pull his ears for being slow at lessons; nor would he have his boy owe a slave so precious a gift as learning. So he made himself the boy's school master, just as he taught him the laws of Rome and bodily exercises; not merely to throw the javelin, to fight in armour or to ride, but also to use his

fists in boxing, to bear heat and cold, and to swim against the currents and eddies of a river. And he tells us himself that he wrote books of history with his own hand and in large characters, so his son might be able even at home to become acquainted with his country's past.[11]

However, in Rome as in Greece this noble educational ideal proved to be a difficult one to implement due to the influx of slaves, the disintegration of family life and the demands of the expanding Roman empire in the third and second centuries B.C. More and more, from that time onward, parents began hiring tutors for their children, or sending them to schools modeled on the Greek schools. Roman elementary schools, however, tended to focus almost exclusively on reading, writing and arithmetic, and the teachers were poorly supported by small fees supplied by the parents. These schools were also poorly equipped and extremely boring, writes Jerome Carcopino, since they met almost every day of the year (except for summer holidays) from dawn to noon, and there was an excess of time to master what little subject matter there was. As a result, he adds, most children carried away "the gloomy recollection of years wasted in senseless, stumbling repetitions punctuated by savage punishments."[12]

Looking at the educational ideals and methods reflected in various texts of the Old Testament in this light, what comparisons and contrasts might one draw so far as educational *goals* are concerned? It seems evident, to begin with, that education for *military* preparedness was not nearly as prominent in biblical culture as it was in Sparta, or even Athens or Rome. In fact, we read nothing in Hebrew scripture about fathers training their sons in the arts of war, or sword handling, or horse riding, or javelin throwing. Also, the cultural goals of Athenian education do not seem to correspond to what we find in Hebrew writings. While parents in Israel might well have taught their children to read and write, it is nowhere said that they did so, nor that they taught them how to play musical instruments or the like.

Rather, the educational goals of the biblical people seem to be closest to those of *ancient* Roman civilization. Proverbs 4 de-

clares, for example, that what the grandfather told the father, and
the father the son, was to cherish wisdom, by which was meant
primarily knowledge of good and evil and how to avoid the path
of evil and choose the good path which, it is said, "is like the light
of dawn, its brightness growing to fullness of day" (4:14). This
text also states that "more than all else" students should keep
watch over their hearts "since here are the wellsprings of life"
(4:23).

What may have been meant by such admonitions, more concretely, is outlined in Psalm 78:3–8 in sentences that read as
though they were crafted as a kind of educational manifesto:

> What we have heard and know,
> what our ancestors have told us
> we shall not conceal from their descendants,
> but will tell to a generation still to come:
>
> the praises of Yahweh, his power,
> the wonderful deeds he has done.
> He instituted a witness in Jacob,
> he established a law in Israel,
>
> he commanded our ancestors
> to hand it down to their descendants,
> that a generation still to come might know it,
> children yet to be born.
>
> They should be sure to tell their own children,
> and should put their trust in God,
> never forgetting God's great deeds,
> always keeping his commands,
>
> and not, like their ancestors,
> be a stubborn and rebellious generation,
> a generation weak of purpose,
> their spirit fickle towards God.
>
> (*New Jerusalem Bible*)

Here then, perhaps, is a kind of overview of educational goals in Israel: first, to learn to know the basics about Yahweh, both what he represents in himself (his "praises" or titles), and what he did by way of past deeds and miracles, as well as what he gave to Israel by way of laws (hence, theology, history, morals)— and all this with the end in view that the children might come to trust in Yahweh and keep his commandments, and in turn pass this knowledge on to the next generation (hence also education, pedagogy).

I suggested above that this ideal and approach would appear to be closest to the educational goals of the ancient Romans, but even in that regard one senses some significant differences. Israelite education was, it seems, much more concerned than was Roman education with cultivating in children, as a first priority, a certain attitude or feeling for *God*, for Yahweh. Hence a religious dimension played a much greater role in education here than elsewhere, it appears.

Most striking of all, however, in comparing Israelite education with that which developed in Rome or Greece, is the degree to which in Israel the ideal of the home as a setting for educating children was realized. While in Israel too there might well have existed publicly funded academies or schools for an upper class elite, during certain periods (in Jerusalem, for example, from the Solomonic era onward), strange to say, such schools are never explicitly referred to in our sources, and what is emphasized instead (in the biblical texts available to us) is the responsibilities that fathers and mothers have for teaching their own children.

In appraising this remarkable fact, the emphasis placed upon *both* parents as the educators of their children should not be overlooked. In the typical Greek family, as just noted, men *only* received an education in the schools, and even in Rome only the father is portrayed as teacher of his sons. By contrast, in biblical tradition children were instructed to listen to the teaching of their fathers *and* their mothers (Prv 1:8; 23:22; 31:26). This too is the point of the commandment which heads the list of social teachings that make up the second part of the decalogue: honor your father *and* your mother (Ex 20:12; Lev 19:3; Dt 5:16). In Israel such respect for both parents was regarded as one of the most important of all biblical teachings, next in rank to the command to honor God himself (see Lev 19:2f).

That fathers *and* mothers were so highly regarded as teachers in Israel implies that the family domicile was being thought of as a classroom of sorts. There where parents shared life on a daily basis with their children was the single most important setting for the education of children into what it meant to be an Israelite. This ideal is put forth with special clarity and passion in the biblical book of Deuteronomy. Of course, it is not the family residence *only* that Deuteronomy focuses on as the bearer of tradition. Communal festivals where laws are recited and covenants made are also identified in this book as having an important part to play in the education of this people (see, for example, Dt 27–28 and 31:9–13). But Deuteronomy seems to imply that it is in the family that education at its best occurs—and this because of the way in that setting instruction can occur at almost any time, while "at rest in your house or walking abroad, at your lying down or at your rising" (Dt 6:7), informally and personally in response to spontaneous questions (see Ex 12:26; 13:14). Here too, in the setting of the home, one is free to experiment in such matters as memorization by means of wall mottos, or the like (Dt 6:9f; 11:18–21).

From this it can be seen why respect for *both* parents was regarded as so important in Israelite culture. This particular educational model requires a home in which a father and mother are present and both are completely familiar and at ease with the religious heritage, so that they can share it in an informal, relaxed and friendly manner in the course of daily life. Needless to say, it was the cultivation of strong, stable, father-involved families that made this educational model possible.[13]

CONCLUDING COMMENTS

This chapter was begun with the suggestion that new modes of fathering began emerging in Israel in the wake of its experience of God as redemptive father. Through the rituals of redemption of the first-born, circumcision and passover, fathers in Israel came to be involved with their families and children to a degree unparalleled in other cultures. In the course of time they also became teachers in their families, again to a degree that was unique. It might be said, in fact, that it was this emerging sense of responsibility for teaching among the Israelite fathers that gave rise to the Hebrew Bible itself. Thus the frequently noted peda-gogical power of Hebrew scripture itself bears potent witness to a new and more vigorous involvement of fathers as caretakers of children in the culture in which this scripture was born.[14]

Eventually public schools *were* established in Judaism too, as elsewhere in the ancient world—at that point, in fact, when the Hebrew Bible had emerged and had begun to assume a para-mount role of its own in Jewish life as sacred scripture. What happened to fathering, then, is the story I will be tracing in the next essay.

Notes

1. On God as father in biblical tradition, see the prior two essays in this volume ("God as Father in the Bible . . ." and "Depatriarchalizing God in Biblical Interpretation: A Cri-tique"), and the literature cited there. The best review to date of human fathering in biblical tradition is the substantial essay by Lothar Perlitt, "Das Bild des Vaters im Alten Testa-ment," in *Das Vaterbild in Mythos und Geschichte*, H. Tellen-bach, ed. (Stuttgart: W. Kohlhammer, 1976), pp. 50–101; but see also Roland de Vaux, *Ancient Israel, Its Life and Institu-tions* (London: Darton, Longman & Todd, 1961), pp. 19–55; E. S. Gerstenberger and W. Schrage, *Woman and Man*, Bibli-cal Encounters Series (Nashville: Abingdon, 1980); James B. Hurley, *Man and Woman in Biblical Perspective* (Grand Rapids: Zondervan, 1981).

2. Regarding the expression "father and mother" and its central-ity and pervasiveness in Israelite tradition, see Perlitt, "Das Bild des Vaters," pp. 60–62, where he writes: "So gibt es

kaum eine Sphäre des Lebens, in der ein Israelit seiner Eltern anders gedächte als in der Gleichrangigkeit und ausdrücklichen Nennung von Vater *und* Mutter" (p. 61).

3. On the exodus narratives seen from this point of view, see the seminal study by Theodor Reik, *Mystery on the Mountain: The Drama of the Sinai Revelation* (New York: Harper & Brothers, 1959), and also my essay, "Psychoanalytic Approaches to Biblical Religion," *Journal of Religion and Health*, 22/1 (Spring 1983), pp. 19–29.

4. Regarding the importance of the story of Abraham's near sacrifice of Isaac for the future of the father-involved family, see chapter 3 of this volume ("Male-Centered Reproductive Biology and the Dynamics of Biblical Patriarchalism"); also, "A Biblical Charter of Children's Rights," in the Appendix.

5. In her study of Jewish child-rearing practices Shoshana Matzner-Bekerman, *The Jewish Child: Halakhic Perspectives* (New York: KTAV Publishing House, 1984), discusses the ceremony of the "Redemption of the First-Born" under the general heading of "Welcoming the New-Born" (Chapter 4). My comments on contemporary practice are indebted to her description of this ceremony, pp. 56–59.

6. For a succinct, authoritative summary of what is known about this ritual both from biblical and extra-biblical sources, see Roland de Vaux, *Ancient Israel*, pp. 46–48.

7. Felix Bryk, *Circumcision in Man and Woman: Its History, Psychology and Ethnology* (New York: American Ethnological Press, 1934), pp. 181–187.

8. Roland de Vaux, *Ancient Israel*, p. 47.

9. *The Jewish Child*, pp. 45–51.

10. William Barclay, *Train Up a Child: Educational Ideals in the Ancient World* (Philadelphia: Westminster, 1959). See also I. F. Dobson, *Ancient Education and Its Meaning to Us* (New York: Cooper Square Publishers, 1963); A. G. Beck, *Album of Greek Education: The Greeks at School and at Play* (Sydney: Cheiron Press, 1975); Stanley F. Bonner, *Education in Ancient Rome* (London: Methuen & Co., 1977).

11. The source of this quotation is Plutarch's *Cato Major* as quoted by Barclay, *Train Up a Child*, p. 155.

12. Jerome Carcopino, *Daily Life in Ancient Rome: The People and the City at the Height of the Empire* (New Haven and London: Yale University Press, 1940), p. 107.
13. Carol Meyers in "Procreation, Production, and Protection: Male-Female Balance in Early Israel," *Journal of the American Academy of Religion*, LI/4 (December 1983), pp. 569–593, has assembled an impressive array of archaeological and textual evidence pointing to a high degree of equality among men and women in Iron Age Israel. She believes that the account of the creation of woman in Genesis 2 was written to provide ideological support for this state of affairs.
14. Walter Brueggemann makes a similar point in *The Creative Word: Canon as Model for Biblical Education* (Philadelphia: Fortress, 1982), p. 15. In the exchanges between parents and children alluded to in such texts as Exodus 12:26; 13:8, 14, Deuteronomy 6:20–21, and Joshua 4:6, he writes, "are the starting point for the literary, *canonical* process, as well as for the *educational* process." This "manifest concern for the educational process," he says, may be regarded as "the taproot of the completed form of the Torah."

7

NEW MODES OF HUMAN FATHERING
(NEW TESTAMENT)

While highly supportive of the biological father-involved family, New Testament Christianity was more focused, it seems, on fostering the growth and development of vital spiritual families under the leadership of spiritual fathers and God as father.

A glance at the book of Acts where the origins of Christianity are chronicled will indicate that Christianity began as a sect of Judaism, and only gradually emerged as a religion in its own right. In other words, the immediate background of the New Testament was not the Old Testament, but Judaism as it was beginning to develop in first century Palestine. This being so, before turning to an analysis of what New Testament scripture has to say on the topic of fathering (the subject of this essay), it may be useful to note what was happening to father roles generally in the Judaism of this period.

FIRST CENTURY JUDAISM

An important point to remember is that the Hebrew scriptures (Old Testament) were now a firmly entrenched religious authority, especially the Torah (first five books of Moses). All first century Jewish sects regarded the laws and traditions enshrined there as divinely revealed truth that required zealous study and application in daily life. As a consequence schools and traditions of interpretation had already sprung up that would eventually rival in authority the scriptures themselves. It was in this way that there emerged those compendia of rabbinic insights and teachings, the Mishnah and Talmud, which were eventually to become as sacred to the Jews as were New Testament writings to Christians. While the final editions of Mishnah and Talmud were not completed until long after the New Testament was written, it seems likely that many of the traditions referred to there were in place among at least some Jewish groups already during the period when Christianity was being born.[1]

What then do we learn from these documents regarding the way the role of the father might have been developing within certain sectors of the Judaism of this period? Were there any new trends emergent, any new emphases? Fortunately, we do not need to guess at the answer to these questions, for there is a section of the Talmud devoted explicitly to this issue. In the talmudic tractate Kiddishun, beginning with section 29a, there is a passage on the duties of fathers, where it is indicated that the rabbis of old had devoted much thought to such matters and had arrived at a consensus which specified that, with respect to a son, a father has five responsibilities: first, to circumcise him; then to redeem him (if the eldest son); third, to teach him Torah; fourth, to teach him a trade; finally, to find him a wife. Some rabbis added that a father should also teach his son to swim!

After stating these duties in outline form, the Kiddushin tractate goes on to discuss each one in greater detail. Special attention is devoted to the importance of the father's role as teacher of Torah and a trade. Both are regarded as essential to the son's future well-being. The duties of a father toward his daughter are also touched upon. She too will need the father's attention and help, especially in finding a husband. The detail and specificity of the document are impressive.

From this document alone it is evident that the father-involved family continued to occupy a central place in Jewish life. It was the primary locus of ritual action and instruction—". . . a continuous, theocentric educational institution," as one scholar has described it.[2] Indeed, even though this was the era when synagogue schools were also begun, these did not replace the role of the father or the family as the primary setting of socialization and learning, but were seen rather as supplementary. This emphasis on the nuclear family and its role in spiritual formation has remained a unique feature of Jewish life and tradition right down to the present.[3]

CHRISTIANITY

It was in a social environment such as this that Christianity was born. In fact, it is not unlikely that it was in such a home headed by just such a Jewish father (as is described in Kiddushin 29a) that Jesus of Nazareth, founder of Christianity, lived and grew to maturity. Such was the case, at least, with that other great figure in the emergence of Christianity, Paul (or Saul) of Tarsus, apostle to the Gentiles (see what he says on this score in 2 Corinthians 11:22). Did then this emphasis on the father-involved family remain a trait of Christianity?

That it did not to the same degree is already hinted at by the fact that there is no single text in New Testament scripture quite like the talmudic tractate we have just looked at. In fact, the paucity of New Testament texts that speak explicitly to or about fathers regarding their duties as fathers *of their own children* is a little surprising. This in itself may be significant, as I will suggest later on. Nevertheless there are New Testament passages that bear *indirectly* on this subject and I would suggest we look at these first of all.[4]

THE GOSPELS

Among passages in the gospels that bear *indirectly* on the role of fathers are the following:

(1) It is well known how Jesus spoke out against easy divorce and remarriage. "What therefore God has joined together, let not man put asunder" (Mk 10:9). Few religious leaders made this point more strongly.[5] In doing so he was also supporting, indirectly, the ideal of lifelong monogamy and the father-involved family, for only as sexual unions are exclusive and enduring can

men even begin to know who their children are, much less be significantly involved in their care.

(2) Jesus' words about the importance of children are also indirectly supportive of fathering in that they are spoken to his male disciples regarding *their* attitudes toward children. Indeed, Mark reports that Jesus was angry at his disciples for their distorted values in this regard. When they rebuked certain parents for bringing their children to him for his blessing (10:14), he told them instead: "Let the children come to me, do not hinder them, for to such belongs the kingdom of God" (Mk 10:14). It was then that he also said that "whoever does not receive the kingdom of God like a child shall not enter it." Following this saying, we are told, he took the children into his arms and blessed them. This act of taking the children into his arms was a prophetic sign dramatizing just how important such children were to him.

A similar point was made on another occasion when these same disciples had been arguing over who would be greatest (Mk 9:34). True greatness, Jesus told them, consists of a servant-like attitude (9:35). Then "he called a little child and had him stand among them" and said: "Whoever receives one such child in my name receives me; and whoever receives me, receives not me but him who sent me" (Mk 9:37). "To receive somebody" always means "hospitality, be it as a temporary guest or through adoption as a permanent member of the family," writes Hans-Ruedi Weber. "Whether he [Jesus] spoke of children in general or referred especially to children of the poor and to orphans is not specified," he adds, but "such hospitality for children and adoption were common practice in the Jewish environment of Jesus."[6] Clear, in any case, is the way this passage equates a receptive attitude toward children with a receptive attitude toward God. By implication neglect or rejection of children is tantamount to a rejection of God. It is hard to imagine how the importance of caring for children could be stated any more forcefully (two Matthean sayings, Matthew 18:6 and 19, make the same point with similar intensity). A caring attitude by males toward children is an absolutely essential trait of the disciple of Jesus.

And yet it must be acknowledged that even here Jesus does

not address fathers explicitly as to their role and duties as biological fathers of their *own* children.

(3) Still another way in which Jesus may be said to have spoken *indirectly* to the issue of fathering is through his own conduct as a man during his public mission. His whole demeanor was that of a certain kind of father. This shines through virtually everything he said and did: his healings, his approach to women, many of his best known stories and sayings. For example, the gospels occasionally preserve phrases in Aramaic (his mother tongue) that were uniquely memorable. One such was his word to a little girl whose parents thought her dead: "*Talitha cum*—little lamb, arise" (Mk 5:41). Why was this tender word preserved in its Aramaic original? Perhaps because it was so characteristic of him. A core memory of Jesus was this authoritative, father-like, yet extremely tender way of speaking and acting. He was a certain kind of father—perhaps the father that many of the alienated of his time had not had and were inwardly secretly longing for.

Jesus likened himself to a physician. "Those who are well have no need of a physician, but those who are sick . . ." (Mk 2:17). In another saying he alludes to himself as a shepherd on a mission to "the lost sheep of the house of Israel" (Mt 10:6). The sick he was trying to heal and the lost sheep he was trying to find were those of his contemporaries who were suffering because they could not cope with some of the new and stricter forms of Judaism then coming into vogue. From the point of view of this new religious elite the people attracted to Jesus were "sinners" and they had to wonder if Jesus himself was not one too (Mk 2:15–17). As a result a controversy developed, one that eventually led to his rejection and death.

But again, through this whole very difficult experience, Jesus remained remarkably firm, even tough and courageous at points, but always with a certain tenderness and grace that was highly touching and memorable, even life-transforming for some who experienced it for the first time. One might say that Jesus himself was a new kind of father—obviously moral and upright, certainly strong, even aggressive, but at the same time humble, compassionate toward sinners, and not as preoccupied with adher-

ence to the details of Torah as were some of his Jewish contemporaries (Mk 7:14–23).

(4) The root of this new "fatherly" approach, Jesus himself
declared in many different ways—and this too has a bearing on
our theme—was a new understanding of the human predicament,
on the one hand, and a new understanding of God, on the other.
As to the human predicament, the whole issue of what defiles
was a crucial one in Jesus' day (see Mk 7:1–23). Certain foods,
contact with the dead, certain bodily emissions and the like were
said in Hebrew scriptures to defile and make unclean. As well,
certain cleansing rituals were prescribed for dealing with these
defilements. Issues of this kind had become very important to
certain sects in the Judaism of his time.

But somehow—and it is another of the little miracles associated with his career—Jesus managed to break free of this type of
thinking without rejecting Torah altogether. His point of view
seems to have been that it is not what goes into a man that defiles,
but what comes out of him, out of the heart (Mk 7:14–16). Simultaneously he grasped afresh, perhaps through his own experience
at his baptism, that by turning sincerely and humbly to God,
even apart from obedience to every last law, God *can* be found
and change of heart and forgiveness can be experienced (Lk 18:9–
14).[7]

The God whom he himself found in this way was tenderly
referred to by him not as master of the universe, or Lord (the
traditional way of addressing God in his time), but as Abba, the
endearing word a small child used in those times in speaking to
his father (or respected adults).[8] This Abba was the God of Israel,
the God of Hebrew scripture, but experienced now again in a
fresh, intimate, fatherly way. How Jesus felt about this God is
movingly expressed in numerous sayings and parables, and especially, of course, in that most moving parable of all, his story of a
prodigal son who was so generously received home by his father
that his more upstanding elder brother was filled with consterna-
tion (Lk 15:11–32).

In this story especially, all that Jesus felt about both God as
father and human fathering found a classic expression. It is some-

thing like this that he had in mind, no doubt, when he said to his male disciples, not: Be *holy*, as the Lord your God is holy (that was the motto of certain contemporary Jewish sects), but: "Be *compassionate* as your Father is compassionate" (Lk 6:36). Marcus Borg, in an important recent study, has referred to this as "the Mercy Code" and believes Jesus was quite deliberate in formulating it as a contrast to the Holiness Code.[9] In Jesus a new, more merciful type of father is revealed—or better, perhaps, revealed *again*, since God's gracious fatherliness is a prominent motif of the Hebrew scriptures as well.

(5) There is yet another piece of gospel data that must be mentioned as of some indirect relevance to this issue of fathering in the New Testament, and that is the fact that during the time of his public mission Jesus was both alienated, apparently, from his parental family (see Mk 3:19b–21), *and* unmarried—hence without an immediate biological family context. This unusual situation may have been due to a personal tragedy. It is quite likely that Jesus' father had died some years earlier, perhaps when he was still a teenager, before the time had come when his father would have arranged a marriage for him had he been alive.

As eldest son Jesus would have then become head of his deceased father's family. It was possibly in that role that he grew to manhood and lived out his life during his later teens and twenties. This, I suggest, may be one of the reasons he never married, and also why when he left this role as his deceased father's surrogate to go out to John the Baptist, and then began his public mission, his mother and brothers and sisters were so surprised and disturbed, at first (see Mk 3:19b–21, 31–35).[10]

Whether or not this hypothesis is correct, something like this must be in the background to explain the degree to which Jesus at this time of his life was in fact both alienated from his parental family and had no alternative biological family of his own. As he viewed it, in fact, the mission he was on, and the people who were gathering around him through his mission, were his *true* family, and were replacing his biological family (Mk 3:31–35).

Thus, already during the mission of Jesus there began to surface that rather sharp bifurcation between the biological family and the spiritual family that has remained a feature of the

Christian movement ever since. It is apparent that for Jesus the spiritual family came first, the biological family second, so that if a tension should arise between them, there is no question as to what choice one must make. To a would-be disciple who wanted to bury his father before following him, Jesus said: "Let the dead bury their dead" (Mt 8:22).

Here, I suggest, is a partial explanation for the lack of attention in the teaching of Jesus to the role of fathers as caretakers of their own children. At the time of his mission Jesus was alienated from his family of origins and without wife or children of his own. He functioned instead as a spiritual "father" in the midst of a growing spiritual family.

In summary, while contributing powerfully to the strengthening of the father-involved family through his passionate sense of God's merciful fatherhood, his vigorous support of marital fidelity and his prophetic words about the importance of children, by failing to speak explicitly to the issue of a father's duties in his own family, and by drawing a contrast between the biological family and the spiritual family, the Jesus of the gospels could be interpreted as downplaying the one against the other. I will have more to say about all this at the conclusion of this essay (and in the concluding essay of this collection).

THE REMAINDER OF THE NEW TESTAMENT

What of the rest of the New Testament? Are these new emphases that we have observed in the life and teachings of Jesus also found there? Do any new trends surface? The picture of fathering in the rest of the New Testament is remarkably consistent with the one just outlined, with a few supplemental touches here and there. The following are a few of the more important points reiterated there.

(1) To begin with, Jesus' unique emphasis on the importance of enduring sexual bonds in marriage is clearly and forcefully represented there as well. In fact, in one of his rare references to Jesus' teachings it is to his sayings about divorce and remarriage that Paul appeals, in seeking to encourage marital fidelity among his Corinthian converts (1 Cor 7:1–11). Paul adds to this, in other

passages, pastoral-type counsel for wives and husbands in the building of their relationship to one another and to their children. Wives should be prepared to defer to their husbands in certain respects, and husbands are encouraged to entertain a certain initiative in loving and caring for their wives (Eph 5:21–33). Whatever one might think of Paul's advice in this sensitive area, he is obviously only intent on one thing: to see that his converts preserve a very high ideal of family life, one where husbands and wives are faithful to each other and function harmoniously and lovingly together in their care of each other and their children (see also Col 3:18–21).

(2) Also, needless to say, what Jesus said about *God* as father and about the graciousness of God, and about finding forgiveness and salvation through faith in this gracious God, is represented elsewhere in the New Testament on almost every page. In fact, one of the foremost features of these scriptures is just this amazing force with which this new understanding of God manifests itself.[11] "Father" has here become God's name, as in the Lord's Prayer: "Our Father, hallowed be thy name. . . ." Indeed, even in the far-off Christian congregations of Rome the Aramaic usage of Abba which had been Jesus' own unique way of invoking God became a distinguishing mark of the Christian movement and a concrete sign that one had become a believer and a Christian (see Rom 8:15; Gal 4:6). Elsewhere Paul regularly refers to this same deity as "the Father of our Lord Jesus Christ." The mighty paean of praise to this God and Father in Ephesians 3:14–21 is just one of many examples of how New Testament scriptures exalt this aspect of the divine revelation that broke into history through Jesus. At the center of New Testament scripture is "the Father from whom every paternity whether spiritual or natural takes its name" (Eph 3:15).

(3) We look in vain, however, in these same scriptures, other than the gospels, for something comparable to Jesus' prophetic words regarding the importance of children.[12] In compensation for this lack, so to speak, we do have there something that is missing in the gospels: a few sayings, at least, addressed specifically to fathers as fathers regarding the fathering of their own

children. Brief as they are, it is impressive to note that these say exactly what (from the indirect evidence we have garnered so far) we might expect to be said on this subject by people who had become followers of Jesus.

The first and shortest of these sayings in Colossians 3:21 is simply a warning to fathers: "Fathers, do not provoke your children, lest they become discouraged." The second, in Ephesians 6:4, repeats this warning, but adds a positive admonition: "Fathers, do not provoke your children to anger, but bring them up in the discipline and instruction of the Lord." Apart from two passing comments in passages devoted mainly to other matters,[13] these are the only statements in the entire New Testament spoken explicitly and directly to fathers as to their responsibilities as caretakers of their own children!

It is not insignificant, perhaps, that what is identified in the first of these sayings as a chief problem in fathering is a certain over-severity or capriciousness that might be discouraging to children or arouse their anger. "Fathers, take care that you not be overly severe." One recognizes in this a continuation of that struggle against the unregulated power of fathers (*patria potestas*) that was begun (within the communities shaped by biblical faith) in the time of Abraham.

In the second of the two sayings devoted to this subject Christian fathers are admonished to play an active role in raising and educating their children. The substance of their pedagogy is defined as "discipline and instruction of the Lord" (Eph 6:4). The phrase "of the Lord" may allude to an instructional tradition originating in Jesus—perhaps the passing on of the kind of stories and sayings that were eventually written down and assembled in our gospels. Unfortunately this is nowhere stated in so many words, nor is any further indication given as to what more precisely an education informed by "the Lord" might entail. Either what was involved was so well understood that nothing more needed to be said about it, or the Christian pedagogical traditions were still vague and in flux. I might note here already, however, that it was vagueness on such issues that predominated as a feature of the Christian movement for the next four centuries,[14] and there remains a certain amount of confusion at this point among Christians right down to the present. I will have more to say on this matter below.

(4) Another indirect way in which the new mode of fathering emergent through Jesus was preserved and perpetuated in the rest of the New Testament was through the teaching there regarding the conduct and demeanor required of men as spiritual leaders of congregations. It was through such leaders especially that the model of fathering exhibited by Jesus himself was chiefly perpetuated in early Christianity.

While passing reference is made to the qualities such leaders should have as fathers in their own families (as for example in 1 Timothy 3:1–3 where it is said that they should be married no more than once and able to elicit obedience from their own children), the focus in this teaching is on their role as spiritual leaders. 1 Timothy 3:1–5, for example, specifies that men who have spiritual "oversight" should be temperate, discreet, hospitable, good teachers, not heavy drinkers, not hot-tempered, but kind and peaceable. A comparable list is cited in Titus 1:7–8: never arrogant, or hot-tempered, nor a heavy drinker or violent, nor out to make money, but a man who is hospitable and a friend of all that is good, sensible, moral, devout and self-controlled. One might assume that such are the qualities as well that are now also being valued for men generally, and for fathers in particular, although this is nowhere said in so many words.

(5) In other words, here too (in the remainder of the New Testament outside the gospels) a certain tension persists between the home and the church, between the biological family and the spiritual family. This tension is strongest in the teachings of Paul, who like Jesus appears to have been without a family of his own during the time of his missionary endeavors, and who, in his earlier writings at least, advocated celibacy as an option for those who were able and suited to it (1 Cor 7:25–40). Certainly Paul does not disparage marriage and family, but it is nevertheless clearly intimated by him that tensions can and do exist between the necessities of family life and the requirements of a devout spiritual existence, and that Paul preferred to see these tensions resolved in favor of celibacy and a life devoted to "pleasing the

Lord" (1 Cor 7:32–35). So in this respect too the trends and emphases emergent in the gospels are perpetuated in the communities of the early church.

(6) There is one point, however, at which Christian thought in the period after Jesus went even further than he did in spiritualizing father-roles, and that is in the Paul-led movement to make circumcision optional as a family ritual among Gentile converts. The circumcision issue is so far behind us today, and biological father-rituals so foreign to our experience, that we forget that Paul's proposals in this regard were for a time the number one issue confronting the early church. It is also often forgotten that in retrospect the decision reached at the famous Council of Jerusalem described in Acts 15 to go along with Paul on this matter opened up an almost irreparable breach between Jews and Christians (initially, in fact, between Christians and Christians). Most Christians to this day appear to have little understanding of why this ritual was of such great importance within Hebrew scriptural tradition, or why their Jewish brothers and sisters cling to it as tenaciously as they do right down to the present.[15]

SUMMARY AND CONCLUSIONS

In summarizing what we have been trying to convey in this essay, it might be said that in Judaism and Christianity two new forms of religious tradition emerged, each springing from and strongly oriented toward the traditions enshrined in Hebrew scripture, yet with somewhat modified modes of fathering. In the one, Judaism, the biblical tradition of fathering was much more closely adhered to and even elaborated. For one thing the father-family rituals were strictly observed (circumcision, passover and redemption of the first-born), and the father-role as teacher of Torah to his children was strongly endorsed and supported. Other tasks essential to the father-role were also delineated (teaching the son a trade, helping his children find spouses, teaching his son to swim).

In Christianity, on the other hand, the ties with Hebrew scripture were a bit looser, although still intact. The visage of the father became more kindly and gracious. At the same time the family was diminished somewhat as the focus or center of religious life through the dropping away of fathering rituals and the shift of priorities to the spiritual family (congregation). The importance of the marital bond continued to be stressed, even more so, perhaps, but with less emphasis on what, in specifics, a father's role should consist of in his own home in relation to his own children. The importance of a receptive attitude toward children generally was powerfully emphasized in a few isolated teachings of Jesus, but only two pieces of advice, concretely, are to be found in the entire New Testament directed to fathers in their role as fathers of their own children. These caution them against being overly severe with their children, lest they become angry, and counsel that they be brought up in the discipline and instruction of the Lord. In this tradition more emphasis was placed on the qualities of men as spiritual fathers (or leaders) of congregations or churches than on their role as biological fathers in their own families.

In trying to explain this shift of focus I have noted the fact that both Jesus and Paul, the principal figures in the emergence of the Christian tradition in the first century, although themselves products of strong Jewish families, were unmarried and without biological families of their own, it seems, at least at the time of their public missions. Their family was thus the community of those who were joining the family of God in the missionary movement of the church.

How shall we assess these developments? I believe they pose important questions for modern North American Christians as they try to cope with one of the most severe family crises since the dawn of the father-involved family. Undoubtedly, Christianity's focus on the spiritual family contributed significantly to its missionary success worldwide. At the same time, deemphasizing the biological family as it sometimes has may make it vulnerable to anti-family pressures in the cultures to which it has spread. This seems to be happening today. I will be commenting further on this subject in my concluding essay.

Notes

1. Regarding this point, see Jacob Neusner, *Self-Fulfilling Prophecy, Exile and Return in the History of Judaism* (Boston: Beacon Press, 1987), p. 68, who writes that "much of the law of the Mishnah derived from the age before the document was completed."

2. Hans-Ruedi Weber, *Jesus and the Children: Biblical Resources for Study and Preaching* (Geneva: World Council of Churches, 1979), p. 40.

3. Regarding this, see Shoshana Matzner-Bekerman, *The Jewish Child: Halakhic Perspectives* (New York: KTAV Publishing House, 1984), pp. 227f.

4. An adequate treatment of the father-role as reflected in New Testament scripture still remains to be written. A beginning on this subject has been made by Levi B. Sommers, in his unpublished dissertation for the Faculty of the School of Theology, Fuller Theological Seminary, *Biblical Perspectives on the Role of the Father* (1980).

5. For an analysis of Jesus' teachings on this subject and their continuing relevance, see my *A Christian Approach to Sexuality* (Scottdale: The Mennonite Publishing House, 1971).

6. Hans-Ruedi Weber, *Jesus and the Children*.

7. For a careful analysis of the important issue of Jesus' attitude toward the Torah see John Bowker, *Jesus and the Pharisees* (Cambridge University Press, 1973), pp. 42–52.

8. On Jesus' unique way of addressing God, and how it compared to the traditions of his time, see Geza Vermes, *Jesus and the World of Judaism* (Philadelphia: Fortress, 1983), pp. 39, 42.

9. Marcus Borg, *Conflict, Holiness and Politics in the Teaching of Jesus* (Lewistown, N.Y.: Edwin Mellen, 1984), pp. 123–134.

10. For an elaboration of this hypothesis and its implications for our understanding of Jesus, see my "Jesus' 'Age Thirty Transition': A Psychohistorical Probe," *Journal of Psychology and Christianity*, 6/1 (Spring 1987), pp. 40–51.

11. Regarding this, see Robert Hammerton-Kelly, *God the Father, Theology and Patriarchy in the Teaching of Jesus* (Philadelphia: Fortress, 1979), who summarizes (p. 88): "God the Father . . .

was the living reality of early Christian experience, the appellation by which that experience was focused and celebrated in public worship and private prayer."

12. In a remarkable piece of exegetical detective work Hans-Ruedi Weber, *Jesus and the Children*, pp. 43–51, documents how the early church even adapted Jesus' own words about "the child," being apparently "more interested in what a child symbolizes than in Jesus' attitude to actual children. This is even more true," he writes, "for the remainder of the New Testament" (p. 49).

13. In an aside, to explain why he was not wanting to be supported by his Corinthian "children," Paul states that children should not have to support their parents, but parents their children (1 Cor 12:14). It is also stated elsewhere that elders must be model fathers who elicit obedience from their children (1 Tim 3:4, 12; Tit 1:6).

14. It is Barclay, *Train Up a Child*, pp. 234–238, who called this to my attention. Not only, he writes, does the New Testament itself have "practically nothing to say about the training of the child" (p. 235), but neither did the early church for the first four centuries. "She provided careful and detailed instruction for her catechumens, and for her ministry, but for her children she provided none at all" (p. 238).

15. According to talmudic teaching, quoted by Shoshana Matzner-Bekerman, *The Jewish Child*, p. 44, "The covenant of circumcision is considered as important as all the *mitzvot* [commandments] in the Torah together." This practice alone explains "the reason for the survival of the Jews throughout their traumatic history." "Time and Byzantium will become but a memory, but the nation which practices circumcision will endure forever."

PART FOUR
CONTEMPORARY ISSUES

Psychological fathering . . . is what the world is in need of more than ever in its history. There is a considerable body of scholarly evidence that civilization will stand or fall with whether such fathering is available in sufficient quantity.*

* Edward V. Stein, "Fathering: Fact or Fable?" in *Fathering: Fact or Fable?* Edward Stein, ed. (Nashville: Abingdon, 1977), p. 11.

THE CONTEMPORARY FATHERING CRISIS: THE BIBLE AND RESEARCH PSYCHOLOGY

Fraught with difficulties in every generation, father-ing today has become especially problematic, due to the impact on father-roles of the modern industrial and sexual revolutions. Yet, modern research psy-chology, in conjunction with the insights and sup-port of biblical tradition, may be on the verge of releasing a new paradigm of fathering that will en-able us to resist and even surmount these trends.

My purpose in this essay is to attempt to indicate how three forces in North American culture—the Bible, research psychol-ogy, and a fathering crisis—are beginning to intersect in a way that could be highly important for our future well-being as fami-lies and as a society.

The Bible, of course, no matter how regarded, has been and still is an imposing "presence" in our civilization. As David Bakan has pointed out, it has "survived the test of the social equivalent of natural selection" by being "reaccepted more regularly and more reliably, generation after generation" than any comparable set of writings.[1]

By contrast, research psychology is an upstart. And yet, as a glance at the advice columns in our daily newspapers will confirm, it too is making its presence felt. For many it has already displaced the Bible as an authority in sexual and family relationships.

The contemporary fathering crisis, I hope to make clear, is only the most recent outbreak of father-deprivation, one of our oldest but still most portentous human problems. My thesis is that research psychology, responding in part to the contemporary fathering crisis, may be on the verge of releasing (in continuity with the Bible) a paradigm shift in our concept of fathering, a shift that could be of positive long-range significance.

But to understand why this may be so, we must begin our discussion, first of all, with several observations regarding the emergence in history of fathering.

THE ORIGINS OF FATHERING

When did men begin fathering their own children? The very question implies that a time existed when this was not the case. This clearly is so, and some awareness of this fact and of the steps that may have led to fathering as we know it today, may afford us a horizon within which better to understand more recent developments.

Students of human culture point out that among the very oldest artifacts of antiquity a pregnant female figure is predominant (dating from the last ice age) and that the fecundity of women became an even more powerful cultural and religious symbol when agriculture was discovered.[2] For it was then that the fruitfulness of the soil was assimilated to the experience of women, and for millennia, Eliade writes, it was thought that Mother Earth gave birth by herself, through parthenogenesis.[3] It is only to be expected that during this cultural phase paternal representations are notable by their absence. A partial explanation seems to be that the role of the male in pregnancy is at this point still imperfectly understood, while the woman's role in the human life cycle is only too apparent.[4]

Hints of what family life may have been like under these circumstances can be derived from observations of matrilineal tribes where the male's role in pregnancy is still unknown.[5] In these societies fathers are thought of as "guests" and the mother and her children (and her brothers) are the primary social unit.

But we can gain an even wider and sharper perspective by noting family patterns among certain highly developed primates, the African chimpanzees, for example ("our closest living relatives," according to anatomical, behavioral, and genetic affinities).[6] Here too a maternal figure is similarly predominant, for within the larger chimpanzee community of from thirty to eighty individuals it is the chimpanzee mother who is responsible for caring both for herself and the children born to her every three or four years (from the time she first becomes pregnant, at eleven or twelve, until she dies some thirty or forty years later). By contrast chimpanzee males spend their adult lives mostly moving about in small groups with other males, apart from the mothers and children, attending to their own needs. They pay little or no attention to their young. Indeed, they have no way of even knowing who their own offspring are, for when mating their contacts with females are brief, promiscuous, and socially inconsequential. It is the family unit of mothers and children that is clearly the chimpanzees' most enduring and important social unit.

The question persists therefore: If a family of this type (one in which mothers are dominant and males are marginal as husbands and fathers) was the historical starting point for the development of the human family, how and when did males begin fathering? One hypothesis is that a first step in this direction may have been taken *within* the kin group of mothers and children.[7] Andrienne Zihlman has proposed that, as early hominids began spreading out over wider territories in search of food, care of the young by the mother alone must have become increasingly difficult. If the maternal group was to remain intact and survive, older male siblings of necessity would have had to help. Selection, she suggests, would have favored those groups where this happened.[8] Since chimpanzee females determine to some extent with whom they mate and are frightened by the rather ferocious approach of some males, another factor in the advent of fathering, Zihlman adds, may have been female preference in sexual coupling for "those males who were more social and less aggressive and were [already] contributing to the welfare of their own kin group."[9] Although Zihlman does not say so, this would suggest that as child-caring males were selected as mates, they simply transferred their instinct for fathering from the maternal kin group to their own offspring.

However, the transition to fatherhood as we think of it today can hardly have been this simple. That additional complexities were involved is clearly intimated by those myths that every-where in antiquity began to displace the earlier maternal myths referred to above. These are stories of heroes, all men, who typi-cally do some great deed, such as slaying a dragon, for which they are rewarded with a female (or females) to mate with from their own age group. [10] *These indicate that as a condition for fathering a certain development had to take place in masculine self-consciousness.* The dragon (or its equivalent) in these myths, Erich Neumann proposes, is symbolic first of all of the mother, and that it had to be killed betrays the degree to which her hold on the psychic life of male children in particular (under the conditions of an increas-ingly prolonged childhood) had become problematic. Before men could begin fathering, a masculine style and identity *apart* from their mothers had to be fashioned, and this occurred, Neumann argues, within the autonomous male groups, led by older males (fathers of sorts), under the conditions of foraging, hunting and fighting that were unique to them. [11]

Just how important this step was to the development of fathering is indicated by the fact that it was during this same period of antiquity that puberty rituals which have played such an enduring role in the human family were fashioned. Their purpose too, we now realize, was quite simply to facilitate the transition of males out of the maternal group to the world of men, and then to families of their own. [12] In addition, the growing awareness (perhaps as animals were domesticated) of the function of the male in reproduction, as well as the phasing out of the female fertility cycle (making possible an increase in sexual relat-ing) must have also played a role (as frequently noted) in men becoming more intimately and lastingly involved with their wives and children.

However, right on down to the present, in the human fam-ily, emotional ties of sons to their mothers continue to be so powerful and the autonomy achieved so tenuous that their relations to their "second families" (that is, to their own wives and children) are frequently fraught with problems. This is the condition that confronts us almost everywhere we turn when we examine more closely the inner dynamics of family life in the great majority of human societies, both ancient and modern. To one degree or another in ancient Mesopotamia, Canaan, Egypt, and Greece,[13] in modern Africa, India, China, and Japan (to mention but a few examples),[14] fathering remains among humans an often precarious, tension-filled role, while females regularly perpetuate the intense maternal traditions exemplified among the chimpanzees. Only through insights arrived at in this century are we now in a position to say, more precisely, why this is so.

But before turning to that, I want to look briefly at the place of the Bible in this unfolding history of fathering.

THE BIBLE AND THE ORIGINS OF FATHERING

Most people today are aware of the fact that the Bible is the literature of a people (Israel) living in close contact with the wider culture of the ancient near east during an axial age spanning roughly two thousand years (the second and first millennia B.C.). So far as fathering is concerned, generally speaking, the matrifocal family is now a thing of the past. Men typically, in these cultures, marry and are husbands of one wife and fathers to their own children.[15]

But it does not follow, as often imagined, that fathers were thereby firmly established by then, or secure as ruling patriarchs in these families. On the contrary, the prevailing stories and myths of the ancient near east often characterize them as weak and ineffective in comparison with their more powerful sons, wives, and daughters.[16] Sons especially are singled out in many of these stories as particularly unsettled and ambitious. Gilgamesh, in the Gilgamesh Epic (a story widely circulated in the ancient near east during the second millennium), is a case in point. He tyrannizes his city with his undisciplined energy before finally setting off with a peer on a long journey of adventure and discovery. Fathers in the story are depicted mostly as watching helplessly on the sidelines.[17] Also, while fathers are everywhere titularly in charge, their rebellious, adventurous sons, not they, are the ones *really* ruling in heaven and on earth (again according to the myths and legends).[18] In short, the ancient near east taken as a whole gives the impression of still languishing in a cultural phase more determined by heroic, somewhat grandiose, militant sons than by confident, effectively caring fathers.[19]

But is this the best that can be hoped for in human family dynamics and culture?[20] It is in answer to this question, I suggest, that the Bible enters the picture. In its pages we read of an ancient near eastern people who broke free of the prevailing myths. And what enabled them to do so, they testify, were events and revelations (Ex 20:2) that persuaded them that the strongest, most benevolent power at work in the universe (and the *one* power therefore to be seriously attended to, Ex 20:3) is neither son, daughter, nor mother, but a unique *father*-God who is compassionately and effectively involved and concerned with the welfare of his children (Ex 34:6f; Dt 32:6; Jer 3:19; Is 63:16; Mal 2:10; Lk 11:2; Eph 3:14f).[21]

Through faith in this God the role of human fathering in the biblical community was gradually transformed. Males, first of all, became more secure (Prv 14:26), and hence less needful of heroics in establishing their identities. To walk humbly with their god, and, like him, to care for others became the male cultural ideal (Mic 6:8).[22] With greater self-confidence (grounded as it was in a source that transcended the family) there came also greater freedom among Israelite sons to "leave father and mother" and become "one" with their wives (Gen 2:24). As a consequence, marital fidelity and love were progressively extolled (Prv 5:18–20; Gen 2:24; Song 8:6f; Mal 2:13–16) and women generally were less feared and more appreciated by men as their "counterparts" or equals (Gen 2:18–23).[23] For this same reason sexual conduct disruptive of marriage (rape, incest, adultery, homosexuality, transvestism, sodomy) was identified and opposed to a degree unprecedented in the ancient near east.[24]

It is only to be expected that children born of such marriages, in the setting of this faith, would also be afforded a protection and care that was equally unique. This expectation can be verified, first of all, through the fact that infanticide, still widespread in ancient times, was abolished by the Israelites (Gen 22:11f; Mic 6:7).[25] But also in less tangible ways Israelite husbands began to complement the child-caretaking roles of their wives. From the beginning in Israel, it seems, fathers thought of themselves as spiritual guardians of their families and symbolized this through their priest-like roles in family rituals such as consecration of the first-born (Ex 13:1f, 11–16), circumcision (Gen 17:9–14), weaning (Gen 21:8), passover (Ex 12:1–14), and unleavened bread (Ex 12:15–20; 13:3–10). Child discipline too was increasingly seen to be the father's rather than the mother's primary task, for, it was said, "the rod and reproof give wisdom but a child left [by a father] to himself brings shame to his mother" (Prv 29:15; cf. 23:13f).

But above all, fathers in Israel became teachers of their children, not primarily in that more sophisticated mode exhibited in the book of Proverbs but through daily contact and informal conversations between themselves and their children (Dt 11:19), prompted more often than not by questions posed by the children themselves (Ex 12:26; 13:14; Dt 6:6–9, 20f). The basic content and purpose of these conversations is movingly summarized in Psalm 78:4–7, where fathers declare that what they had heard from their fathers should be shared with the next generation: namely, the titles of Yahweh, his power, his mighty deeds, and the decrees and laws he has instituted in Israel, all of which, in the telling, they stress, awakens confidence in God and ensures that his achievements and commandments will never be forgotten.

God himself is characterized as just such a compassionate teaching father in Hosea's portrait of the way, when Israel was an infant, he chose him, fed him, embraced him, taught him to walk, and, as Israel grew older, instructed him "with leading strings of kindness and love" (Hos 11:1–4).

It was this paternal passion for teaching in Israel that in the course of time gave birth to a body of literature—the Bible—one which may be characterized, quite simply, as a body of writings produced, for the most part, by fathers for sons or younger fathers, with the purpose, broadly speaking, of instructing them in fathering (or caring).[26] Eventually, through Judaism and Christianity, these writings were disseminated worldwide, and wherever their influence spread, mother, son, and daughter deities faded as consciousness of the divine father grew. This in turn brought about the transformation in masculine attitudes that had given birth to the Bible in the first place: the bonds between men and women in marriage were gradually strengthened, as were men in their roles as caretakers of children.

THE CONTEMPORARY FATHERING CRISIS

During the last century, however, influences have arisen in most modern societies severely challenging these biblically inspired trends. Foremost among these are the industrial revolution and now, in its wake, a far-reaching sexual revolution.

The initial impact of the industrial revolution on family life was devastating, as whole families were herded into mills and factories. But even with the introduction of child labor laws and compulsory education during the nineteenth century, it has continued to make family life difficult in a number of ways. First, due to the necessity now of moving about in pursuit of work, the nuclear family (fathers, mothers, and children) was often dislodged from its extended family network of grandparents, uncles, aunts, and cousins. This weakened the ties between generations and diminished the involvement of older people with younger families.

At the same time the nuclear family itself was reshaped significantly because of the way the place of work was separated from the family residence. In many older societies families worked together, fathers and sons in one sphere, mothers and daughters in another, both in geographical proximity (as is still the case today in family farms and businesses). When during the later phases of the industrial revolution children were kept out of the labor force and sent to school and it became customary for mothers to stay home while men alone (for the most part) went off to work, this had the effect of isolating fathers from wives and children. Under these conditions women, until recently at least, tended to revert to their archaic role of primary caretakers of children while men gravitated to male groups and a sphere of life outside the home. A degree of father-deprivation unknown in many pre-industrial societies was the result.[27]

Into this social milieu burst the sexual revolution in the late 1960s and 1970s. Their ties to family already strained by conditions brought about by the industrial revolution, and spurred on by the availability of birth control devices of one kind or another, males (and females too, of course) began questioning the necessity of confining their sexual activity to one spouse only. In a single decade in North America (between 1971 and 1979) the ideal of sexual celibacy before marriage, until this point a pillar of the American family system, was abandoned as a prevailing cultural norm.[28]

Several consequences quickly followed: marriages became more fragile, divorce rates accelerated, and out-of-wedlock pregnancies increased dramatically.[29] This in turn resulted in an alarming increase in single-parent families, the vast majority of which are mother-led.[30] Another consequence is now also in sight: growing numbers of father-deprived children with overly intense and therefore more problematical maternal ties that endanger their emotional development (more about this later).

It is this combination of trends, I suggest, that constitutes our contemporary fathering crisis. While millions of children are deprived of appropriately caretaking fathers by conditions brought about by the industrial revolution, millions more are virtually being abandoned by fathers caught up in the sexual revolution.

RESEARCH PSYCHOLOGY

It is well known that powerful reactions to this crisis are already in motion and have been for some time. Women themselves (in this century especially) have been fighting back, both by challenging the more devious pursuits of their male counterparts (booze, gambling, pornography) and by pressing for a more autonomous lifestyle and equal rights for themselves.[31] During the last decade (for this and other reasons) they have also been entering the workforce in unprecedented numbers, and this alone has been a critical factor in forcing men to reconsider their roles in family caretaking responsibilities.[32] Even independent of this, however, men themselves, perhaps, disillusioned by their experience in a depersonalized, technologized society, have in recent years been gravitating toward aspects of parental experience often denied them. An especially notable example of this is the growing number of men now sharing more intimately in the birth experience of their wives. It should be noted that in communities inspired by the Bible (church and synagogue), powerful movements have arisen in recent years challenging men as seldom before to pay more attention to their families.[33]

But another important voice, I suggest, is also being heard in the land, one that because of its base in the university and the deference in our culture to scientific authority, may be as important as any. This is the voice of research psychology where an awareness has been growing, in recent years, of the importance of fathering in human personality formation.

At the beginning of this century when research psychology was still in its infancy, Freud already discovered how essential fathers were to the formation of conscience in young children during their so-called oedipal years from three to six (more about this later). But research psychologists were slow to capitalize on these discoveries, partly because of their origins in seemingly (to some) abstruse therapeutic conversations, but also because the society generally was more focused on maternal roles in childcare than on fathering. Even as late as 1965 John Nash, a research psychologist who pioneered in the study of father-roles, could lament the lack of concern about fathering on the part of his peers and attribute this to little or no interest in the subject in the culture at large.[34] Since then, however, there has been a dramatic change. Psychological research on fathering has mushroomed during the last two decades, so much so that it has already generated a remarkable set of insights, some of which are beginning to inform the actions of increasing numbers of parents.[35]

Of these, broadly speaking, two stand out, I believe, as of very special importance for the future of fathering: the first having to do with *when* fathers should ideally become involved in parenting their children, the second with *how*.

As to when: Freud's breakthrough discovery (already referred to) of the father's role in conscience formation had already alerted researchers to the fact that paternal involvement in children's lives was essential quite early if they were to grow up able to "work and love," at least as early as the oedipal years from four to six. A wealth of recent studies not only confirms this judgment,[36] but suggests that fathering is important even earlier, indeed from birth onward. This research of course in no way diminishes the well-established fact that mothers too play an irreplaceable role in the lives of infants and young children. Their capacity for unique emotional closeness and sensitivity in caring (conveyed through countless acts of feeding, smiling, talking, caressing) are in fact decisive in establishing that bedrock of security and trust in children that is foundational for everything else.[37]

But what is clear now is that fathering too, during this very same period, has an equally important *complementary* contribution to make in at least three ways:

First, by simply being there as a significant "second other" for their infants to relate to, fathers can help them, even during their very first months, to put distance between themselves and their mothers and so make a solid beginning on the road to maternal separation and individuality.[38]

Second, fathers are also virtually indispensable in helping their children control and come to terms with their still wildly fluctuating aggressive impulses, during their "terrible twos" especially, when internal ego-controls are still fragile.[39]

Third, through their special sensitivity and concern for gender distinctions fathers contribute immeasurably to the crucial formation of firm body-congruent gender-identities in both sons and daughters.[40] This, we now realize (and it is among the most important psychological discoveries of recent times), does not happen automatically. Gender itself, of course, is a biological given, but gender-identities are formed in response to subtle distinctions in parenting (many of them father-initiated) during the eighteenth to twenty-fourth months of children's lives, before, in most instances, children can even talk.[41]

A particularly sobering illustration of the importance of fathering in this earliest age period (1–3) is provided by what is now known about the origins of homosexuality in men. Since

Freud the search for the genesis of this disorder has consistently pointed to a pattern of parenting, early in life, characterized by weak or absent fathers and over-involved mothers. Freud, however, focused on the way this pattern makes it difficult for boys to identify with their fathers during the oedipal years (3–6). More recent research underlines the impact of such parenting on children even earlier. Socarides, for example, reports that two-thirds of the approximately four hundred adult homosexual men he has counseled suffered from a blurring of the boundaries between themselves and their mothers and acute gender confusion, and this is due, he writes, to an experience with "crushing mothers" and "abdicating fathers" already during the very earliest pre-oedipal years of their lives. "The father's libidinal and aggressive availability," he writes, "is a major requirement for the development of gender identity in his children, but for almost all prehomosexual children the father is unavailable as a love object for the child."[42]

So urgent is a child's own felt need for a father during these first years that one researcher has termed it "father hunger"[43] and another likens the father in his role at this time of his children's lives to that of a lifeguard rescuing a child desperately trying to reach shore while being pursued by a dragon.[44] In this light it is not insignificant perhaps that the first word children say, typically, is not mama, but daddy (or its equivalent) and the first picture that absorbs them is again his, not the mother's.[45] When men abandon their families at this age and stage, it is not unusual for their children to have terrifying nightmares from which they awaken screaming for their fathers.[46]

But not only has research psychology, in recent years, underscored the importance of an *early* involvement of fathers with their children, it has also begun to generate a number of insights regarding the *kind* of fathering that is needed. This facet of the research is best illustrated, perhaps, by what is now seen to be required of fathers during the oedipal years from three to six. It is then, as Freud first pointed out, that children typically entertain romantic thoughts and emotions toward the parent of the opposite sex, while experiencing competition, even hatred, toward the same-sex parent. For children to have such emotions is an important step in self-discovery, for it is through this that they can begin to visualize their potential for becoming men and women with a procreative and parental destiny of their own. However, to realize that potential, children must also rather quickly begin to undergo an emotional transformation whereby they let go of the opposite-sex parent and become reconciled with the parent of the same sex, thereby internalizing the renunciation of incest and murder—the core of a healthy conscience. Both to affirm these ascendant oedipal emotions but then also to facilitate their transmutation are among the most complex and consequential challenges confronting the nuclear family.[47]

In the case of a boy, Freud thought, the lever that brought about these important changes (that is, the eventual detachment from the mother and rapproachement with the father) was fear of being castrated by the father should he persist in the maternal attachment. This indeed is a factor in some instances, but then, too, identification with the father will often turn out to be precariously ambivalent. This is the inner condition that typically presents itself in counseling with adult male neurotics, where paternal affection, if present at all, is often interlaced with resentment, and the tie to the mother is still strong. A major development in recent research is the verification that this is by no means the only, nor even the optimal way that the resolution of the oedipal drama may proceed. Boys with firm but also friendly and supportive fathers have a much easier time identifying with them and letting go of their mothers than boys with fathers who are too stern and disciplinarian.[48]

Girls too during this oedipal period can derive a great deal of self-confidence from their fathers, if, once again, the fathers are not just strong, but warm and supportive. Girls, however, in contrast to boys, must eventually desexualize the paternal tie and let go of their competitive posture toward the mother if they are to recover an identity more in line with hers and marry someone in their age group.[49] This requires, on the father's part, in addition to his encouraging stance, a certain reserve, if he is not to inhibit her development at this crucial stage. Even so, as Lora Tessman points out, the "remnant attachments" of her love for him are sometimes not completely swept away until the daughter herself is married and her rapprochement with her mother may need to await the time when she has given birth to a child and is secure in a maternal role of her own (this because of regressive fears that mothers can reactivate in both sons and daughters).[50]

Even these few comments should make it clear that fathering, especially from the oedipal years onward, is a complex and subtle task with important long-range consequences. As to the kind of fathering that is needed, at least four characteristics may be deduced from the above observations: to father well, fathers must be (1) involved, (2) assertive and strong (rather than passive), (3) affectionate, and (4) capable of fostering a loving bond between themselves and their wives.

That they should be involved should be obvious, but unfortunately has not been, especially not that the father's involvement is of very special importance during their children's earliest years. Assertiveness and strength are required above all to foster autonomy and counteract the tendency of mothers and children to hold on to each other (as well as his daughter's attachment to him).[51] Affection, as just noted, facilitates the paternal identifications and attachments of both boys and girls so necessary to their sexual identities and self-confidence. Finally, a father's bond with his wife insures the fulfillment of their own sexual-emotional needs in such a way that generational distinctions are firmly maintained and their children's efforts at having one or the other for themselves alone (the essence of the oedipal situation) are frustrated.[52] At the same time it provides a model for children of what they may look forward to when they are older and ready to get married themselves.

The father's role in the life of his children does not end with the oedipal years. During latency (seven to twelve) he continues to be needed as friend, mentor, and guide, and during early adolescence his loving firmness, if present, will again serve as a shield and support for the working through of the autonomy and role-identity issues that first surfaced in his children during their oedipal years.[53] Only as children marry and become parents themselves does the paternal role begin to shift significantly from that of caretaker to something more akin to facilitator. However, even then, with the advent of grandchildren, an "unambivalent admiration and love of young children" (as one researcher has put it) may be powerfully revived, energizing fathers (now grandfathers) to complement in significant ways the parenting provided by their own now adult children.[54]

It is with these psychological benefits and realities in mind that Antoine Vergote, a leading religious psychologist, has aptly characterized the father as the primary agent in our progessive humanization.[55] And this too is why Edward Stein, another religious psychologist, has written that the presence of the right kind of fathers in sufficient numbers, during the coming years, may well determine whether our civilization will stand or fall.[56]

A PARADIGM SHIFT

At the beginning of this essay I wrote of a paradigm shift in our concept of fathering that may be coming to birth through the conjoint midwifery of the Bible and psychology. In this concluding section I will try to clarify more precisely in what sense this might be true.

The Bible, it was stated earlier, through its revelation of God as effectively caring father, may be viewed as fostering, within the broad sweep of history, a generally stronger, more confident, more faithful type husband and father. However, viewed in the light of what is currently known about fathering through research psychology, it can be seen that even the Bible is not as clear, at some points, as we now realize we must be if fathering is to be optimally effective. The two issues just discussed in the previous section are a case in point: *when* fathering is important, and *what kind* of fathering it is.

Concerning the "when" of fathering, it will be recalled that, like research psychology, the Bible also, in certain passages, emphasizes the importance of fathers becoming involved with their children *early* in their lives. However, nowhere does it specify *how* early, and this, as we have seen, is an issue of considerable consequence. It is tragically evident, in fact, in the light of what is now known, that fathers in most cultures (whether biblically influenced or not) become meaningfully involved with their children *too late*. Already at five, for example, maternal over-investment, coupled with paternal deprivation, may have had such a disturbing effect on a child's emotional development that it will suffer from it for the rest of its life. In highlighting the importance of fathering for children already during the very first years of their lives, research psychology has given precision and force to the biblical maxim that promises that if fathers take an interest in their children while they are still children and direct them in the way they should go, they will not depart from it even when they are old (Prv 22:6).

However, similarly unclarified in the Bible, in some respects, is the issue of what kind of fathering is needed. While rightly stressing *both* forcefulness *and* friendliness as paternal modes, it must be admitted that a certain ambivalence attaches to the biblical portrait of fathering, an ambivalence which has lent itself to a variety of interpretations and cultural expressions. More specifically: a certain pedagogical severity in fathering may be garnered from certain texts (Prv 22:15; Heb 12:7–11), while a more relaxed, compassionate fathering is gleaned from others (Ps 103; Eph 6:4).[57]

The place of corporal punishment in childrearing may serve to illustrate the issues at stake. Several biblical passages advise a generous use of the rod without specifying more precisely how generous, at what age, or under what circumstances (Prv 22:15; 23:13; 29:15). How at least some fathers in Israel interpreted this counsel (and not the least intelligent ones either) can be seen in the redoubtable Jesus ben Sirach's stern words on parenting. If a father truly loves his son, he writes, he should avoid playing with him or sharing his laughter, but rather be strict with him, correct his mistakes, bend his neck, bruise his ribs, and beat him frequently (Sira 30:1–13).

As noted, research psychology also emphasizes that fathers should be assertive and firm but intimates as well that the kind of firmness that may be called for during the "terrible twos," for example, may not necessarily be appropriate at five, six, or sixteen, and that children of any age, when punished too much, or where paternal friendliness is missing as a basic mode, may have difficulty relating to their fathers as positively as they should if they are to experience that bond with them that is so essential to their healthy emotional development. Again, therefore, the insights of research psychology lend credibility to certain biblical emphases while also helping us appropriate them with greater finesse.[58]

Needless to say, as the women's movement of our time is reminding us, a third point at which the Bible is somewhat deficient has to do with its relative neglect of both mothering and the father's role in the life of daughters. It would be wrong, however, to interpret the biblical emphasis on father-son relations as necessarily prejudicial to women, in the light of what is now known of the importance of a secure self-identify in men as a precondition of their ability as adults to respect women generally and to marry and become caretaking fathers. But certainly a gap in our knowledge is being supplied by the increasingly vivid picture being painted in research psychology of the complementary roles of fathers and mothers in childrearing and, more particularly, the father's significant contribution to the emotional well-being of his daughters as well as his sons. As this is more widely understood, it may help ease the anxieties of those women who fear that biblical father-religion may somehow be detrimental to their own best interests. On the contrary, as we now know, good fathering facilitates good mothering and contributes to the humanization of both men and women.[59]

These are some of the ingredients I see in the paradigm shift in our concept of fathering alluded to earlier. *On foundations laid by the Bible, research psychology is helping us see not only that fathering is important but that it is important early in the life of children in modes that are firm but friendly—for daughters as well as sons.*

It might be noted in conclusion that if it is true, as the evidence suggests, that such fathering, when it is present, helps children grow up more confident, more capable of working selflessly and creatively, better able to marry and care for their own children, then this only confirms the biblical promise that those shall live long in the land who have available to them a parent of this kind, along with a mother, to honor, and respect (Ex 20:12).

Notes

1. David Bakan, "Paternity in the Judeo-Christian Tradition" in Allan W. Eister, ed., *Changing Perspectives in the Scientific Study of Religion* (New York: J. Wiley, 1974), p. 204.
2. See Mircea Eliade, *A History of Religious Ideas*, Vol. 1, *From the Stone Age to the Eleusinian Mysteries* (Chicago: University of Chicago Press, 1978), pp. 20–22, 40–44.
3. *Ibid.*, p. 40.
4. On this point and its importance for the development of the family, see David Bakan, *And They Took Themselves Wives: The Emergence of Patriarchy in Western Civilization* (San Francisco: Harper & Row, 1979), p. 27; also Chapters 2 and 3 of this volume.
5. See Bronislaw Malinowski, *The Father in Primitive Psychology* (New York: W.W. Norton, 1927).
6. Adrienne Zihlman, "Motherhood in Transition: From Ape to Human," in Warren B. Miller and Lucile F. Newman, eds., *The First Child and Family Formation* (Chapel Hill: Carolina Population Center, The University of North Carolina, 1978), p. 37. The description that follows is based largely on her sketch of chimpanzee society which she believes provides "the most specific beginning for hypothesizing the characteristics of the population immediately preceding the early hominids" (p. 37).
7. *Ibid.*, p. 47.
8. *Ibid.*, p. 48.
9. *Ibid.*
10. On these myths see Erich Neumann, *The Origns and History of Consciousness*, Bollingen Series XII (New York: Pantheon Books, 1954); Joseph Campbell, *The Hero with a Thousand Faces*, Bollingen Series XVII (Princeton University Press, 1949); S.N. Kramer, *History Begins at Sumer* (Philadelphia: University of Pennsylvania Press, 1956), pp. 224–226; Mircea Iliade, *A History of Religious Ideas*, pp. 284–289.
11. On the male group as "the birthplace" of masculine consciousness, individuality and "the hero" see Erich Neumann, *The Origins and History of Consciousness*, pp. 140–145.

12. The antiquity of these rites is stressed by Eliade, *A History of Religious Ideas*, p. 25; also their association with the era of the "heroes" and the beginning of the monogamous family, *ibid.*, pp. 285f. On their continuing importance in many primitive tribes as a means of bringing to an end the son's bond with his mother, see William N. Stephens, *The Oedipus Complex: Cross-Cultural Evidence* (New York: The Free Press of Glencoe, 1962).

13. The way the typical Greek father of antiquity neglected his wife and children (and the consequences of this) are fully documented by Philip Slater, *The Glory of Hera: Greek Mythology and the Greek Family* (Boston: Beacon Press, 1968). According to L. Delaporte, *Mesopotamia: The Babylonian and Assyrian Civilization* (London: Alfred A. Knopf, 1925), p. 85, men seem to have frequently divorced their wives and abandoned their children in that region as well. How this affected their role in the family is reflected in the marginal roles fathers play in Mesopotamian myths and legends. The same is true of the fathers of Canaanite and Egyptian myths. On this see J. W. Miller, "God as Father in the Bible and the Father Image in Several Contemporary Ancient Near Eastern Myths: A Comparison," *Studies in Religion/ Sciences Religieuses*, 14/3 (Summer 1985), pp. 347–354 (Chapter 4 in this volume). The strengths and weaknesses of the typical Egyptian father are carefully delineated by Jan Assmann, "Das Bild des Vaters im aletn Aegypten," in G. Bornkamm, et al., eds., *Das Vaterbild in Mythos und Geschichte* (Stuttgart: Kohlhammer, 1976), pp. 12–49.

14. For Africa, see H. Collomb and S. Valantin, "The Black African Family," in J. Anthony and C. Koupernik, eds., *The Child and His Family* (New York: J. Wiley, 1970), pp. 359–388; for India, see Sudhir Kakar, "Father and Sons: An Indian Experience," in Stanley Cath, et al., eds., *Father and Child: Developmental and Clinical Perspectives* (Boston: Little, Brown, 1982), pp. 417–442; for China, Japan, and other examples see the summaries in David B. Lynn, *The Father: His Role in Child Development* (Monterey, California: Brooks/ Cole Publishing Co., 1974), pp. 33–44.

15. See R. Harris, "Women in the Ancient Near East," in *The Interpreter's Dictionary of the Bible*, Supplementary Volume (Nashville: Abingdon, 1976), pp. 960–963.
16. See n. 13 above, n. 18 below. This point is often overlooked in feminist discussions of "patriarchy" (so-called). For example, Naomi Goldenberg in *Changing of the Gods: Feminism and the End of Traditional Religions* (Boston: Beacon Press, 1979), p. 37, states that "all recorded history has been patriarchal" and therefore only today (in the wake of the feminist movement) are we about to see "what happens when father-gods die for an entire culture. . . ." The truth is that the father-gods were not altogether alive and well even under patriarchy.
17. See N. Sandars, *The Epic of Gilgamesh* (Middlesex: Penguin Books, 1960), for an idiomatic translation and introduction to this story. On its psychological aspects see Thorkild Jacobson, *The Treasures of Darkness: A History of Mesopotamian Religion* (New Haven: Yale University Press, 1976), pp. 218f.
18. The deities vested with ruling the earth in the ancient near east (except for Israel) were all sons (not fathers): Marduk in Mesopotamia, Baal in Canaan, Horus in Egypt. According to E.O. James, *The Worship of the Sky-God: A Comparative Study in Semitic and Indo-European Religion* (University of London: The Athlone Press, 1963), p. 8, father-deities tend to be *Deus otiosus* and marginal to the cult "everywhere in primitive states of culture both in the present and the past."
19. Samuel Kramer, *History Begins at Sumer* (see n. 10 above), p. 224, characterizes the "Heroic Ages" in Sumer, Greece, India, and northern Europe as "essentially barbaric," dominated as they were by princes with retinues of armed followers prepared to do their bidding without question "no matter how foolhardy and dangerous the undertaking."
20. At the conclusion of his study of Greek civilization, P. Slater, *The Glory of Hera* (see n. 13 above), poses a similar question (see p. 462).
21. The massive data bearing on the representation of God as father in the Bible is reviewed by Robert Hamerton-Kelly, *God the Father: Theology and Patriarchy in the Teaching of Jesus* (Philadelphia: Fortress, 1979). Relevant to this subject are

not only those texts where the term father itself is used, but the characterization of God as "God of the fathers" and "father of the gods" through the transfer to him of the name of the Canaanite father-deity "El" (Gen 33:20; Jos 22:22), as well as many El-epithets. See J. J. M. Roberts, "El," in *Interpreter's Dictionary of the Bible*, Supplementary Volume, pp. 255–258. Indeed, many scholars now believe that "Yahweh" (the most often used biblical name for God) may have originated as a cultic epithet for El (Ps 10:12). However, in striking contrast to Canaanite El, Yahweh is "the jealous one" for "a jealous god (el) is he" (Ex 34:14; cf. Ex 20:5; Dt 5:9; 32:16; Jos 23:19; Num 25:11). This energetic paternal emotion is at the root of the monotheistic focus that sets biblical religion apart from all other religions of the ancient world (Ex 20:3; Dt 5:7). See Walter Eichrodt, *Theology of the Old Testament*, Vol. 1 (Philadelphia: Westminster Press, 1961), p. 210, n. 1. Recent feminist claims that the biblical God was also thought of as "mother" are based on several passages where he is characterized as engaging in mother-like activities or as having mother-like attributes. On these see P. Trible, "God, Nature of, in the OT," in *The Interpreter's Dictionary of the Bible*, Supplementary Volume, pp. 368f; Virginia Ramey Mollenkott, *The Divine Feminine: The Biblical Imagery of God as Female* (New York: Crossroad, 1983). A father, however, does not become a mother when likened to a mother, any more than he becomes a rock when likened to a rock (Dt 32:18). Against Sallie McFague, *Metaphorical Theology: Models of God in Religious Language* (Philadelphia: Fortress Press, 1982), "father" is not simply one metaphor among others in the Bible; it is what God in actuality is for his worshipers (Eph 3:14). According to Jesus "father" is his *name* (Lk 11:2; Jn 17:6, 11, 12, 26).

22. The absence of "hero" themes (so prominent elsewhere in the literature of the ancient near east) in the patriarchal stories in Genesis is noted by Claus Westermann, *The Promises to the Fathers: Studies in Patriarchal Narratives* (Philadelphia: Fortress Press, 1980), p. 35. On the father generally in the Old Testament, see Lothar Perlitt, "Der Vater im alten Testament," in

Bornkamm, et al., eds., *Das Vaterbild in Mythos und Geschichte*, pp. 50–101.

23. Concerning the relatively "high status" of women in the Old Testament, see John H. Otwell, *And Sarah Laughed: The Status of Women in the Old Testament* (Philadelphia: Westminster Press, 1977); also Hans Walter Wolff, *Anthropology of the Old Testament* (Philadelphia: Fortress Press, 1974), pp. 169–173.

24. Incest (Lev 18:6–18), transvestism (Dt 22:5), adultery (Ex 20:14), homosexuality (Lev 18:6–18), sodomy (Lev 18:23) are all proscribed in the legal codes. The Israelite attitude toward rape is expressed in Tamar's protest: "Such a thing is not done in Israel" (2 Sam 13:12). On these "disorders of love" (as he refers to them), see again Wolff, *ibid.*, pp. 173–176.

25. On the historic importance of this achievement alone, see E. Wellish, *Isaac and Oedipus: A Study in Biblical Psychology of the Sacrifice of Isaac; The Akedah* (London: Routledge & Kegan Paul, 1953).

26. Concerning the way narrative tradition in the Old Testament arose from paternal instruction in the family, see E.S. Gerstenberger and W. Schrage, *Woman and Man* (Nashville: Abingdon, 1980), p. 35.

27. On these developments see Alexander Mitscherlich, *Society without the Father: A Contribution to Social Psychology* (New York: Harcourt, Brace & World, 1963); and John Nash, "The Father in Contemporary Culture and Current Psychological Literature," *Child Development*, 36 (1965), pp. 261–297.

28. According to a Johns Hopkins University study (reported in an Associated Press release, *Kitchener-Waterloo Record*, October 20, 1980), sexual activity among girls, 15–19, increased to 49.8 percent in 1979 (from 30 percent in 1971); among teenaged males (17–21) 70 percent had engaged in sex.

29. According to government statistics out-of-wedlock births in the United States increased 50 percent during the decade of the 1970s. In 1979 one in six American babies was born to an unwed mother (55 percent of all black babies). At the same time about half of all new marriages are now ending in divorce with 60 percent of these involving children.

30. According to Benjamin Schlesinger, *One-Parent Families and Their Children in Canadian Society* (The University of Western Ontario, 1979), p. 89, 10 percent of Canadian families are now one-parent families (involving 850,000 children), with 83 percent of these being mother-led (without fathers). The statistics for the United States are: 14 percent one-parent families (involving 11,311,000 children), 84 percent without fathers. George Miller in an article entitled "Children and the Congress: A Time to Speak Out," *The American Psychologist*, 38 (January 1983), p. 75, writes that "by the end of the decade there is projected to be a 14 percent increase in the number of children under 10. Close to half of these children can expect to live with only one parent at some time during their childhood."

31. Judith Herman, *Father-Daughter-Incest* (Cambridge and London: Harvard University Press, 1981), p. 213, writes that "many of the causes that women have supported most passionately in the last century—temperance, animal rescue, the suppression of vice—can best be understood as attempts to get men out of the barroom, the game pit, the whorehouse, and into the home."

32. It is estimated that in the United States over one-third of all mothers (35 percent) with children under three are now working outside the home, and that by the time these children are six this percentage almost doubles. See Ross D. Parke, *Fathers* (Cambridge: Harvard University Press, 1981), p. 104.

33. James Dobson, a Christian child clinician who heads up one of these movements, writes in his book, *Straight Talk to Men and Their Wives* (Waco, Texas: Word Books, 1980), p. 21, of having received a revelation to the effect that "if America is going to survive the incredible stresses and dangers it now faces, it will be because husbands and fathers again place their families at the highest level on their system of priorities, reserving a portion of their time and energy for leadership within their homes!"

34. John Nash, "The Father in Contemporary Culture" (see n. 27 above), pp. 264–267.

35. For reviews of the recent research see Henry Biller, *Paternal*

Deprivation: Family, School, Sexuality, and Society (Lexington, Massachusetts: D.C. Heath and Company, 1974); David B. Lynn, *The Father: His Role in Child Development* (see n. 14); Michael Lamb, ed., *The Role of the Father in Child Development* (New York: John Wiley & Sons, 1976); Ross D. Parke, *Fathers* (see n. 32); Stanley Cath, et al., eds., *Father and Child* (see n. 14).

36. See Seymour Fisher and Roger Greenberg, *The Scientific Credibility of Freud's Theories and Therapy* (New York: Basic Books, 1977), especially pp. 396–399.

37. The research on mothering is reviewed by Rudolph Schaffer, *Mothering* (Cambridge: Harvard University Press, 1977). On "maternal sensitivity" as a centrally important characteristic in fostering security and healthy infant development see especially pp. 79–83.

38. See Richard Atkins, "Discovering Daddy: The Mother's Role," in Cath, et al., *Father and Child* (see n. 14), pp. 139–149; Stanley Greenspan, " 'The Second Other': The Role of the Father in Early Personality Formation and the Dyadic-Phallic Phase of Development," *ibid.*, pp. 123–138.

39. See James M. Herzog, "On Father Hunger: The Father's Role in the Modulation of Aggressive Drive and Fantasy," *ibid.*, pp. 163–174.

40. For a review of the research on gender-identity in boys see Phyllis Tyson, "The Role of the Father in Gender Identity, Urethral Eroticism, and Phallic Narcissism," *ibid.*, pp. 175–187; for girls, see Nancy Chodorow, *The Reproduction of Mothering: Psychoanalysis and the Sociology of Gender* (Berkeley: University of California Press, 1978). Henry Biller's earlier study is also still important: *Father, Child and Sex Role: Paternal Determinants of Personality Development* (Lexington, Massachusetts: Heath Lexington Books, 1971).

41. The research leading to this breakthrough discovery is reviewed by Ethel Person and Lionel Ovesey, "Psychoanalytic Theories of Gender Identity," *Journal of the American Academy of Psychoanalysis*, 11 (1983), pp. 203–225.

42. Charles W. Socarides, "Abdicating Fathers, Homosexual Sons: Psychoanalytic Observations on the Contribution of

the Father to the Development of Male Homosexuality," *Father and Child* (see n. 14), p. 512.

43. James Herzog, "On Father Hunger" (see n. 39).

44. Stanley Greenspan, " 'The Second Other' " (see n. 38).

45. Linda Gunsberg, "Selected Critical Review of Psychological Investigation of the Early Father-Infant Relationship," in Cath, et al., *Father and Child* (see n. 14), p. 76.

46. James Herzog, "On Father Hunger" (see n. 39). pp. 154f.

47. For a review of the research on boys' developmental journey during these years, see John Ross, "From Mother to Father: The Boy's Search for a Generative Identity and the Oedipal Era," *Father and Child* (see n. 14), pp. 189–203; for the girl, see Lora Tessman, "A Note on the Father's Contribution to the Daughter's Ways of Loving and Working," *ibid.*, pp. 219–238.

48. This research is reviewed and summarized by Fisher and Greenberg, *The Scientific Credibility of Freud's Theories and Therapy* (see n. 36). In their concluding summary they write that "it is true that experimental studies have shown not only that castration anxiety is common but also that it is incited by sexual fantasy. That much conforms to theoretical expectation. But the evidence is quite convincing that what motivates the boy to identify with the father and his masculinity is not fear but rather father's nurturant friendliness. The boy apparently gives up his competitive struggle with the father because his positive, friendly attitude invites one to become like him."

49. On this see especially Marjorie Leonard, "Fathers and Daughters: The Significance of 'Fathering' in the Psychosexual Development of the Girl," *International Journal of Psychoanalysis*, 47 (1966), pp. 325–334.

50. Lora Tessman (see n. 47), p. 231.

51. Antoine Vergote has written in *The Parental Figures and the Representation of God: A Psychological and Cross-Cultural Study* (The Hague, Paris, New York: Mouton Publishers, 1981), p. 193, that for this reason the father ideally represents "prohibitive law" for both sons and daughters, while the mother's authority is ideally "referential" (to the father). If she im-

poses herself on the child with a direct authority as "judge,"
this may contradict her availability and produce emotional
disturbances. It is striking, Vergote summarizes on p. 189,
that "judge" is the only factor that characterizes the mother
figure of the schizophrenic, a fact that concurs with the clinical data according to which the father of the schizophrenic
does not assume his paternity.

52. On this point see Theodore Lidz, "The Family as the Developmental Setting," in James Anthony and Cyrille Komper-
nik, eds., *The Child and His Family* (New York: John Wiley &
Sons, 1970), p. 29.
53. On father-roles during latency and adolescence see John
Ross, "Mentorship in Middle Childhood," in S. Cath, et al.,
eds., *Father and Child* (see n. 14), pp. 243–252; Charles
Sarnoff, "The Father's Role in Latency," *ibid.*, 253–264; Aar-
on Esman, "Fathers and Adolescent Sons," *ibid.*, pp. 265–
274.
54. Calvin Colarusso and Robert Nemiroff, "The Father in Mid-
life Crisis and the Growth of Paternal Identity," *ibid.*, pp.
315–327.
55. Antoine Vergote, *The Religious Man: A Psychological Study of
Religious Attitudes* (Dublin: Gill and Macmillan, 1969), p.
179.
56. Edward Stein, "Fathering: Fact or Fable?" in E. Stein, ed.,
Fathering: Fact or Fable? (Nashville: Abingdon, 1977), p. 11.
The research indicating that fathers play an important role in
determining children's moral development is reviewed by
Esther Blank Greif, "Fathers, Children, and Moral Development," in Michael Lamb, ed., *The Role of the Father in Child
Development* (see n. 35), pp. 219–236.
57. On this ambivalence and the way it has been variously interpreted from culture to culture see D. A. Köberle, "Vatergott,
Väterlichkeit and Vaterkomplex im christlichen Glauben,"
in Wilhelm Bitter, ed., *Vorträge über das Vaterproblem in Psy-
chotherapie, Religion und Gesellschaft* (Stuttgart: Hippokrates,
1954), pp. 14–26.
58. Research psychologist Bruce Narramore's comments on
spanking in his book *Help! I'm a Parent* (Grand Rapids:

Zondervan, 1972), pp. 83–87, are an example of the way biblical texts on this subject are now being interpreted and appropriated with the help of contemporary psychological insights.

59. Further to this point see J. W. Miller, "In Defense of Monotheistic Father Religion," *Journal of Religion and Health*, 21 (1982), pp. 62–67 (Chapter 9 in this volume); also Antoine Vergote, *The Religious Man* (see n. 55), pp. 167–197.

IN DEFENSE OF MONOTHEISTIC
FATHER RELIGION

*Viewed in the light of its capacity to support and
encourage healthy personal growth to maturity for
both men and women (as this is illuminated by key
insights from developmental psychoanalysis)—and
considering the alternatives—faith in God as caring
gracious father appears to be an optimal form of
religion for both men and women.*

THE PROBLEM

In biblical religion (and consequently western religion) worship
rises to a solitary, transcendent, benevolent father. This is true of
Christianity no less than Judaism. Although Christianity has
sometimes been described as a "son" religion, it is nevertheless
that of a son who mediates to the father (1 Tim 2:5).[1] Many
questions, however, are now being raised about the religious,
social, and psychological effects of such an exclusive emphasis on
God as father. Women especially are increasingly concerned
about the possible detrimental impact of such a religion on their
lives in particular. Would their needs not be better met, they are
asking, if this highly patriarchal focus were modified, either by
introduction of a corresponding matriarchal element, or by aban-
doning the patriarchal image altogether?[2]

In this brief essay I propose to examine this question from the
point of view of certain key insights from developmental psychoanalysis. Viewed in this light, I shall argue, monotheistic father

religion may be more supportive of the emotional well-being of women (as well as men) than it is sometimes portrayed to be.

PSYCHOANALYSIS

The justification for a developmental psychoanalytic approach to this issue lies in the illumination that has come to us from that source concerning the respective roles of father and mother in the emotional maturation of children.[3] They are by no means the same for boys and girls, and therein lies a critical and often neglected element in the current debate.

For boys, a key phase in their progress to maturity, according to psychoanalysis, is the sometimes rather traumatic transfer of affection and trust from the mother to the father during the so-called oedipal years from three to six. Thus by the sixth year of life, the boy typically acquires a secure masculine identity, is liberated for a non-incestuous, guilt-free sexuality, and goes on eventually to become a husband and father in his own right.[4] The girl, too, at about the same time in life, also detaches herself from her mother by means of a trusting, loving relationship to the father. But for her this relationship marks not the end but only a passing phase in her journey to maturity. It is crucial to her emotional development that she move beyond the father, in a kind of oedipal loop, as Gail Sheehy has called it, back to an identity more in line with her mother.[5] Were she to remain with the father, she, like the boy who is tied to his mother, would find herself caught up in an incestuous web that would inevitably inhibit her identity as a woman and her freedom for sexual love.[6]

These few observations already allow us to draw at least two conclusions regarding the way monotheistic father religion typically intersects with key phases in the emotional development of children:

1. Insofar as both boys and girls must put emotional distance between themselves and their mothers, as a first step in reaching maturity, and insofar as the father in both cases plays a significant role in that "individualizing" process, invoking God as benevolent father may be viewed as playing a constructive, supportive role in the psychological formation of both sexes.

2. However, insofar as women, in contrast to men, must at a certain point move beyond the father to complete their identity, the evocation of God as father, in their case, could have an inhibiting effect at this stage in their development.

This would suggest that patriarchal monotheism does indeed confront us with a dilemma. While it offers an emotional environment uniformly helpful to men in surmounting their most crucial and difficult developmental challenge (rapport with the father), it could have a retrogressive effect on women by threatening to anchor them still deeper in an oedipal tie to the father that must eventually be terminated if they are to come into their own. This, I suggest, is the crux of what needs to be dealt with in the current debate in western religion over the gender of God.

PRESUPPOSITIONS

In dealing with the debate, however, attention must be paid first of all to certain basic presuppositions of the religious tradition we are talking about. These are, I suggest, that God is personal and one and is to be worshiped as such by both men and women. *This means that so far as this religion is concerned any recommendation regarding the gender of God must be evaluated from the point of view of its overall capacity to mediate a meaningful unified personal reality to both sexes.* This obviously restricts the alternatives that might be considered. Excluded by these presuppositions, for example, would be the now frequently advocated androgynous option, for there is simply no solid basis in human experience for relating to a *personal* reality that is both male and female, or neither, or fluctuates between the two.[7] If God is "person" and that person is one, only two figures have an analogous "ultimacy" in actual human experience to that of God, and they are mother and father.[8] And while these personages overlap, they are not the same: at crucial points in the emotional journey of children (during the oedipal years especially) they are required to play distinct, complementary roles. To fulfill their respective tasks in the human life cycle fathers must be fathers and mothers mothers. *Thus, a choice must be made, in a personal monotheistic faith, between father or mother as the ultimate symbolic configuration.* The only question then is which it shall be. Are there psychodynamic factors that would favor one over the other as the preferred religious environment for *both* sexes? I think there are.

DEFENSE

To begin with, because of the chronological and experiential primacy of the mother in the birth and initial care of children, a son's emotional bond with his mother is typically more intense than a daughter's tie (during the oedipal years) with her father. As a consequence, it is emotionally more traumatic for a son to achieve a secure sense of male identity and become oedipally liberated than for a daughter. Father religion is, therefore, of more critical importance as an emotional support system for men than mother religion is for women. At the same time, and for the same reasons, mother religion is more threatening to masculine identity than father religion is for the identity of women.[9]

However, it would be quite wrong if this observation were to leave the impression that women should forgo mother religion and more or less endure father religion for the sake of men only. Actually, mother religion is not an altogether favorable emotional environment for women either.[10] While it is true, as noted above, that women need to break free from their fathers and find an identity more in line with that of their mothers, this can happen in a truly meaningful way, as already noted, only *after* they have been freed from an overly dependent maternal bond through a good relation with the father. And even then, women do not typically reidentify with the mother in an emotional, wholehearted way (as, say, the son does with the father) because of the threat of a renewed loss of independence. The role of the mother in helping her daughter find her identity is therefore an important but, at the same time, a restricted one. Other factors are of equal or even greater importance.

I refer in particular to the roles that men play in feminine identity formation, a subject often overlooked in feminist discussions of this topic.[11] The point I now want to make is this (in summary): Not only must men face a more difficult challenge than women in resolving their own oedipus complex, but it is of paramount importance that they do so because of the key roles they must play (as both fathers and husbands) in helping women resolve theirs. I have already called attention to the rather complex process by which women typically form and then terminate their bond with the father and then move on to become women and mothers in their own right. I have also noted that this requires, in the first place, a father who can (during the oedipal years) relate to his daughter in affirming but non-incestuous, non-binding ways. I have not emphasized, however, how important it is, if a father is to play this role appropriately, that he has himself worked through his own oedipal emotions and established an uninhibited sexual relation with his wife. Otherwise the danger is great that he will foster a relationship with his daughter that is characterized by the same incestuous dependencies that tie him to his mother.[12]

Even with the best of fathering, however, the daughter's bond with her father has a tendency to linger—in part this is because of the already mentioned threat to her independence that is involved in any renewed identification with her mother.[13] More often than not, therefore, her tie to the father is terminated (and her status as a woman in her own right confirmed) only when she is "courted" and married and becomes a mother herself.[14] But this, too, requires men who are oedipally liberated, for those whose maternal bond is still strong and whose identification with the father is tenuous invariably turn out to be either insecure and anxious, and as a result frightened of women, or tyrants desperately intent upon proving themselves. *Nothing is more devastating for the emotional well-being of women than such men. While this psychic condition is what some writers seem to have in mind when they castigate western father religion, this is in fact the situation that prevails where the role of the father is tenuous and threatened by matriarchy.*[15]

Authentically secure fathers, rather, foster oedipally liberated males capable of courting and loving women in a manner that frees them from parents for an enduring marital relation of truly autonomous persons. Furthermore, a mature husband in a vital bond with his wife, far from prolonging the emotional tie with his daughter, will actively foster her freedom. In providing, as it does, an emotionally supportive milieu for the attainment of these utterly essential goals, monotheistic father religion, I suggest, may be viewed as an optimal form of religion not only for men, but for women as well.

IMPLICATIONS

It is beyond the scope of this brief essay to spell out the implications of these observations for the actual functioning of men and women in a community devoted to a benevolent father deity. But in concluding it might be noted that in the light of the above at least some of the practices of both Judaism and Christianity may not be as onerous as they are sometimes portrayed. That, for example, in both communities women have traditionally not been at the emotional focal points of worship and leadership is not necessarily to be interpreted as implying an inferior status on their part. Rather, with the previously mentioned psychoanalytic observations in mind, this could be seen as the expression of a healthy sensitivity to the fact that it is, generally speaking, in everybody's best interest, in a father religion, for the women to be more detached and objective in their spirituality.[16] It is the men who must be challenged to lift up "holy hands" in prayer (1 Tim 2:8), not only for their own good but for the sake of the women whose emotional freedom is so vitally dependent on theirs.

Notes

1. On the patriarchal focus of both Jesus himself and canonical Christianity, see Robert Hamerton-Kelly, *God the Father: Theology and Patriarchy in the Teaching of Jesus* (Philadelphia: Fortress, 1979), pp. 52–99.

2. For an astute bibliographical survey and analysis of the discussion of these issues, see Carol P. Christ, "The New Feminist Theology: A Review of the Literature," *Religious Studies Review*, 3 (1977), pp. 203–212.

3. Concerning the current scientific status of psychoanalytic thought, see especially S. Fisher and R. Greenberg, *The Scien-*

tific Credibility of Freud's Theories and Therapy (New York: Basic Books, 1977).

4. Verification of the importance of the son's identification with the father for sexual identity and adult heterosexuality is extensive, even though Freud's understanding of *how* this identification comes about has been shown to be in error at points. Again, see Fisher and Greenberg, *Scientific Credibility*, pp. 170–254.

5. G. Sheehy, *Passages: Predictable Crises of Adult Life* (New York: Bantam Books, 1977), p. 161.

6. On this critical but often neglected point, see M. Leonard, "Fathers and Daughters: The Significance of 'Fathering' in the Psychosexual Development of the Girl," *International Journal of Psychoanalysis*, 47 (1966), pp. 325–334. In her summary she writes that "following the oedipal conflict, the girl must establish a desexualized object-relationship to her father, enabling her later to accept the feminine role without guilt or anxiety and to give love to a young man in her peer group" (p. 332).

7. This would appear to be Carol Christ's conclusion as well. In a criticism of Mary Daly's *Beyond God the Father* (Boston: Beacon Press, 1973), she writes that "feminists are not likely to be satisfied with Daly's symbols of 'androgynous' humanity and God as the 'Verb.' A premature envisioning of an androgynous future will not assist the new becoming of women": "The New Feminist Theology," p. 206.

8. Son or daughter deities either mediate to the parents or displace them. If they displace them, they become the agents of a growth-inhibiting neurosis. This, of course, was a burning issue for early Christianity in its christological controversies. On the psychological dynamics involved, see T. Reik, *Dogma and Compulsion: Psychoanalytic Studies of Religion and Myths* (New York: International Universities Press, 1951), pp. 24–161.

9. Concerning the overwhelming power of the incestuous tie, for men especially, and the way religious and social forces may compound it, see especially E. Fromm, *The Heart of Man* (New York: Harper & Row, 1964), pp. 95–150, and *The*

Anatomy of Human Destructiveness (Greenwich, Conn.: Faw-
cett Publications, 1973), pp. 300–481.

10. Many feminist writers, without explaining why, seem to
concur. Patricia Doyle, for example, in an essay on "Women
and Religion: Psychological and Cultural Implications," in
R. Reuther, ed., *Religion and Sexism: Images of Women in the
Jewish and Christian Tradition* (New York: Simon & Schuster,
1974), p. 32, writes that "in an ecologically sensitive age,
Mariology as well as Mother Earth religion may be appeal-
ing, and worthy of resuscitation. I expect, however, that
many (and not just feminists) would find exclusive association of divinity with motherhood as confining and tyranni-
cal as the father image many now try to escape, so that the
task is to find imagery that transcends sex-specific capacities
and awareness."

11. The outstanding exception to this criticism is Nancy Chodorow's *The Reproduction of Mothering: Psychoanalysis and the Sociology of Gender* (Berkeley: University of California Press, 1978),
where she argues eloquently that the father's role is essential
to the well-being of *both* sexes and that, therefore, he should
play a much larger role than is currently customary in *primary* parenting.

12. On this point Marjorie Leonard, "Fathers and Daughters," p.
332, comments as follows: ". . . when the daughter reaches
the phase in her development when she is searching for a love-
object, the ability of the father to respond to her needs de-
pends on the extent to which his own oedipal conflict is resolved. He cannot give her desexualized affection if his
counter-oedipal response provokes inappropriate defense mea-
sures which will then be reciprocated in his daughter's response. Thus, neurosis in the parent is perpetuated in the
child."

13. Freud thought that fear of loss of love and disappointment of
oedipal wishes provided the chief motivation for the termina-
tion of this tie to the father in girls; but because such motives
do not have the strength of castration fear in men in their
relation to the father, the overcoming of the oedipus complex
is much more problematical and incomplete in many women.

Freud wrote, "Girls remain in it for an inderterminate length of time; they demolish it late and, even so, incompletely." *New Introductory Lectures on Psychoanalysis*, vol. 2 (New York: Penguin Books, 1973), p. 163. On this important issue see also V. Machtlinger, "Psychoanalytic Theory: Preoedipal and Oedipal Phases with Special Reference to the Father," in M. Lamb, ed., *The Role of the Father in Child Development* (New York: John Wiley and Sons, 1976), pp. 277–305.

14. Christ, "The New Feminist Theology," p. 211, seems to be saying something similar when she writes of her discovery that "the experience of motherhood, properly approached, can function for women in ways analogous to the mystic's dark night of the soul, as a time of purgation and integration which opens the self to spiritual experience." Maybe this is the intuition that informs that rather quaint early Christian insight that women "will be saved by childbearing . . ." (1 Tim 2:15).

15. For elaboration and confirmation of this point I refer again to the writings of Erich Fromm, especially his discussion of "Malignant Aggression" in *The Anatomy of Human Destructiveness*, pp. 300–481.

16. Admittedly the roles prescribed for women in the New Testament are viewed there as the result of a certain characterological inferiority on their part ("she is to keep silent, for Adam was formed first, then Eve; and Adam was not deceived, but the woman was deceived and became a transgressor" (1 Tim 2:12–14). A psychoanalytic perspective opens the door for a more positive interpretation of the feminine role in a patriarchal society.

CONCLUSION

The dreariness of the family's spiritual landscape passes belief. It is as monochrome and unrelated to those who pass through it as are the barren steppes frequented by nomads who take their mere subsistence and move on. The delicate fabric of the civilization into which the successive generations are woven has unraveled, and children are raised, not educated.*

*Allan Bloom. *The Closing of the American Mind* (New York: Simon & Schuster, 1987), p. 57.

10

WHICH WAY AHEAD?
(A FEW MODEST PROPOSALS)

Ideals basic to western democracies, such as equality and freedom, have had a corrosive effect on the father-involved family. Christianity too has not always been as supportive of the biological family as it might be, due to its preoccupation with the needs of the spiritual family. The contemporary family crisis is forcing us to reconsider what biblical tradition might contribute to the recovery of a high culture of fathering.

The exceptional fragility of the father-involved family in North America today may have roots that go deeper into our cultural history than we realize. Some researchers believe that the contemporary crisis of the family can be traced back to the writings of the seventeenth century philosopher John Locke, whose ideas laid the foundations for the beginnings of democracy on this continent. In his treatises on government Locke sought to undermine the divine right of kings by challenging the traditional role of fathers in families. His argument was that the very notion of special or privileged paternal power was suspect. Since the mother "has an equal title" to that of the father, he wrote, we should speak of *parental* power instead.[1] He went on to suggest that paternal power so little belongs to the father by some "peculiar right of Nature" that when he quits his care of his children "he loses power over them. . . ." He saw the truth of this insight being verified "in those parts of America where, when the husband and the wife part, which happens frequently, the children are all left to the mother. . . ."[2] For Locke, in other words, the insight that paternal power is weak and without support in "Nature" becomes an argument for its overthrow! "At least from that time to the present," writes the religious psychologist David Bakan of Locke's philosophical critique of patriarchy, "the centrality of the family organization has been declining."[3]

This suggests that the intellectual climate of our western democracies may be more hostile to family values than is sometimes realized. "Freedom" and "equality" (the watchwords of our democratic culture) are not adequate categories for grasping what is going on or needed in this realm. While fathers and mothers are both parents, their "titles" (to use Locke's expression) are not equal, and a too great stress on personal freedom alone is obviously destructive of the very foundations upon which the two-parent family is built.

I refer again to the elementary fact that fathers, biologically speaking, are marginal to the reproductive process. It is the mothers who become pregnant and give birth; it is they who nurse at the breast. Since *nature* invests mothers with such power and preeminence in the human life-cycle, *culture* must intervene on behalf of fathers if they are to be equally (and as significantly) involved. The legal, religious, social and psychological means by which societies have done this have varied from culture to culture. But any civilization that fails to do *something* in this regard will inevitably witness the demise of the father-involved family and a drift toward families headed by mothers alone—precisely as John Locke observed, and as we see happening in America today to an unprecedented degree.

Until recently the spiritual and emotional soil that nourished the father-involved family on the North American continent was the Bible. My intention in these essays has been to heighten the awareness of how these biblical traditions have and still can foster a high culture of fathering. My hope is that by regaining a better perspective on the way "biblical faith and fathering" intersect, we will be encouraged and empowered to continue to appropriate the insights of this tradition in support of contemporary family values.

With this in mind I will conclude with a few suggestions directed to Christians in particular for doing just that. What does a study of the fathering traditions of the Bible contribute to our current struggles in this regard?

A FEW MODEST PROPOSALS

One of the more important consequences of the research done in the preparation of the essays of this volume for me personally has been the dawning realization of the degree to which early Christianity, in breaking free of its Jewish moorings, tended to deemphasize the importance of the biological family in favor of the spiritual family (see Chapter 7). It was this shift in part, no doubt, that enabled Christianity to succeed so magnificently as a missionary religion within and beyond the boundaries of Judaism. Through its evangelism Christianity brought the spiritually homeless into spiritual families headed by spiritual fathers and God as father. In this way the legacy of biblical faith was spread far and wide.

In the process, however, were the needs of biological families neglected? Did Christianity in its break with Judaism lose something in this regard which was never fully recovered? Have, for example, Christians ever found an adequate substitute for the abandoned rituals of circumcision, redemption of the first-born, or passover? Of course, alternative family-related rituals were fashioned such as baptism and eucharist. Baptism and eucharist, however, are rituals of the church presided over by priests or pastors, not rituals of the family presided over by the father. It is doubtful therefore that these rituals perpetuate that link between faith and fathering that is such a strikingly novel feature of Hebraic biblical tradition.

Right here, it seems to me, might be one of the reasons why the Christian church is as vulnerable as it has been to the modern crisis of the family. Being aware of this weakness (if such it is) may be a first step in recovering a richer tradition of support for the father-involved family.

STRENGTHS

With these comments I do not mean to suggest that Christianity has neglected the family. This is obviously not the case. There are many ways in which Christians have been supportive of fathering. These strengths need to be identified, retained and enhanced. The following are a few examples of what I have in mind:

(1) Most Christians still do direct their worship to a God named and thought of as gracious all-powerful father. We still pray, "Our Father, hallowed be thy name. . . ." I hope these essays will have encouraged those who want to uphold this tradition of worship in the face of pressures to do otherwise. I join Diane Tennis in urging: "Do not abandon God the Father. . . . A reliable Father God is a source of judgment on unreliable sexual arrangements, a source of hope for women and for the fatherless, a symbol emerging out of our loss, luring itself in to existence."[4]

(2) Another strength of the churches so far as fathering is concerned is its theology of sex and marriage, and its many wonderful marriage rituals and ceremonies. Let us guard against every tendency to weaken these theologies and traditions. Let us keep on warning of the dehumanizing consequences of sexual relating outside of a permanent lifelong marital commitment. Let us plead for the rights of children to grow up in the atmosphere of such bonded, covenanted two-parent families.

(3) We still do value children and symbolize this in various ways in the church: by our sacred ceremonies for infants; by the way we bring children with us to our worship assemblies; by sitting together as families; by our Sunday schools; by our youth ministers and summer camps; by our alternative schools, church related high schools and colleges. All this is important and should be vigorously retained and supported.

(4) Fathering is still highly regarded among us. A day for

honoring fathers has been added to one honoring mothers in the annual cycle of fifty-two Sundays. Let us be vigilant in the use of this and other occasions to highlight the importance of fathers and fathering. "Fathering is a mark of a redeemed community," writes Diane Tennis. "The Christian community is without excuse for contributing to the absence or perversions of fathering. The Christian community must at minimum reorder its own life to give priority to fathering."[5]

(5) I lamented above the absence of rituals of the family in Christian tradition, but there is one tradition that is still alive in many Christian homes that might qualify as such, and that is the practice of prayer before meals. Fast foods and the pace of modern life are eroding the quality of our mealtimes. Nevertheless, we still do eat together, and as we do, let us be sure to keep this tradition alive. I would urge fathers especially to take a leadership role at this point and not let the responsibility for mealtime prayers fall by default to wives or children, as I have sometimes seen happening.

WEAKNESSES

There are also areas of weakness, I sense—needs that are not being met, or at least not being met nearly as well as they might be. The following are a few thoughts about gaps in the parental support-systems of our churches that I have thought of in the course of writing these essays.

(1) Existent church rituals need to be studied to see how they could be shaped and made more explicitly supportive of parenting roles in the family, the role of the father especially. In Christian marriage ceremonies, for example, little reference is usually made to the roles of husbands and wives as parents. Even in our child dedication ceremonies we tend to focus more on the child than on parental tasks and responsibilities. William Johnson Everett in a recent book suggests that in addition to wedding

ceremonies we need rituals that will help couples envision the parental role as a spiritual vocation—some public declaration of parental intentions, celebrated and solemnized at the time of the birth of a couple's first child, perhaps.[6]

(2) A ritual for children entering the teenage years may be needed in some churches. In a provocative book, *Momism, the Silent Disease of America*,[7] Hans Sebold points to the dearth in American culture of rituals marking the transition from childhood to adulthood, such as the Jewish *bar mitzvah*. The church of which I am a part fashioned such a ritual for its youth some years ago. These teen-entry celebrations, as we call them, are held in homes, and bring parents, grandparents, friends and relatives together to rejoice, reminisce and reflect on the life of the specific young person involved: what she (or he) is becoming; what lies ahead in the near and more distant future. A Bible is given, scriptures are read (the story of Jesus at twelve), hymns are sung, prayers are offered, but it is not a religious commitment that is being celebrated on this occasion, but a young person's arrival at a new and important stage in life: the threshold of adulthood.

(3) Another need in our churches, I sense, is for some quite specific guidance for fathers regarding what they are responsible for in the family (a document not unlike the one in the Jewish Talmud noted in Chapter 7). In a book entitled *Mothers Are People Too* Anita Spencer seeks to develop just such an outline of duties for both fathers and mothers. Following the lead of Hans Sebold she calls them "A Healthy Motherhood Script" and "A Healthy Fatherhood Script."[8] In her "Healthy Fatherhood Script" she includes such items as genuine willingness to extend fathering, active involvement in home chores, and educational preparation for the father role. While her suggestions are a bit vague (compared to the talmudic text, Kiddushin 29a), that such documents are being worked on at all is a hopeful sign that a new day may be dawning in the churches so far as the father-involved family is concerned.[9]

CONCLUDING COMMENTS

It should not be assumed, however, that the crisis of father-lessness now confronting us in North America will be easily surmounted. Harvard University researcher Samuel Osherson, in a recent book entitled *Finding Our Fathers: The Unfinished Business of Manhood*, writes that the interviews he has had with men in their thirties and forties has convinced him "that the psychological or physical absence of fathers from their families is one of the great underestimated tragedies of our times."[10] As I worked on the final draft of this volume, I chanced upon the following passage in Allan Bloom's highly acclaimed study, *The Closing of the American Mind:*[11]

> The fact that there is today a more affirmative disposition toward childbearing does not imply that there is any natural impulse or compulsion to establish anything like a traditional fatherhood to complement motherhood. . . . Ninety per cent or more of children of divorced parents stay with their mothers, whose preeminent stake in children has been enhanced by feminist demands and by a consequent easy rationalization of male irresponsibility. So we have reproduction without family—if family includes the presence of a male who has any kind of a definite function. The return to motherhood as a feminist ideal is only possible because feminism has triumphed over the family as it was once known, and women's freedom will not be limited by it. None of this means returning to family values or even bodes particularly well for the family as an institution. . . .

I must reluctantly agree with this somber analysis. And yet, along with others, I continue to hope that the tide might be turned, for it is altogether certain that should the father-involved family continue to disintegrate as it has over these past several decades, we will face increasingly unmanageable emotional and social disorders and our civilization will repeat the tragic pattern of decline and fall that so many others, for similar reasons, have experienced.[12]

Notes

1. John Locke, "An Essay Concerning the True Original Extent and End of Civil Government," in *Great Books of the Western World*, Robert Maynard Hutchins, ed. (Chicago: Encyclopaedia Britannica, 1952), p. 36.
2. *Ibid.*, p. 38.
3. David Bakan, *And They Took Themselves Wives: The Emergence of Patriarchy in Western Civilization* (San Francisco: Harper & Row, 1979), p. 174; see also Jay Fliegelman, *Prodigals and Pilgrims: The American Revolution Against Patriarchal Authority, 1750–1800* (Cambridge: Cambridge University Press, 1982), p. 4.
4. Diane Tennis, *Is God the Only Reliable Father?* (Philadelphia: Westminster, 1985), p. 9. For compelling evidence of the way feminizing God intersects with and reinforces "father-ineffective" family structure, see Michael Carrol, *The Cult of the Virgin Mary: Psychological Origins* (Princeton University Press, 1986).
5. *Ibid.*, p. 114.
6. William Johnson Everett, *Blessed Be the Bond: Christian Perspectives on Marriage and Family* (Philadelphia: Fortress, 1985), pp. 126f.
7. Hans Sebold, *Momism: The Silent Disease of America* (Chicago: Nelson Hall, 1976), pp. 81–83.
8. Anita Spencer, *Mothers Are People Too: A Contemporary Analysis of Motherhood* (New York/Ramsey: Paulist Press, 1984), pp. 60–65.
9. For an excellent study resource, see also Gordon MacDonald, *The Effective Father* (Wheaton: Tyndale House, 1977). MacDonald identifies six principles for effective fathering, the first being the simple recognition that this is "one of my life's highest priorities. . . ."

10. Samuel Osherson, *Finding Our Fathers: The Unfinished Business of Manhood* (New York: The Free Press, 1986), p. 4.

11. Allan Bloom, *The Closing of the American Mind* (New York: Simon & Schuster, 1987), p. 105.

12. For a sobering analysis of the way father-deprivation in Germany brought about by World War I contributed to the formation of the Nazi Youth Cohorts which became the foundation for Hitler's rise to power and the traumatic events leading up to World War II, see Peter Loewenberg, *Decoding the Past: The Psychohistorical Approach*, "The Psychohistorical Origins of the Nazi Youth Cohort" (New York: Alfred Knopf, 1983), pp. 240–283.

APPENDIX

A BIBLICAL CHARTER
OF CHILDREN'S RIGHTS:
GENESIS 22

Jewish tradition refers to the story told in Genesis 22 as "the binding of Isaac," and regards it as a work of art and theological insight of a very high order, a classic of the rank of Jesus' parable of the lost son. Regarding it the noted biblical scholar E. A. Speiser has written (in his Genesis commentary) that it records "perhaps the profoundest personal experience in all recorded history and the telling of it rises to comparable literary heights."[1] In its opening line it refers to God "testing" Abraham as to whether he would be willing to offer up his son as a blood sacrifice, but what follows hints at something far greater: Abraham's step by step personal transformation, culminating in the revelation that this was not what God wanted of him after all.

It was not, then, Abraham's willingness to offer up his son, in and of itself, that is the focus of this account (in that respect Abraham was simply a child of his time), but the whole process by which he responded to this "test" and finally arrived at the point where it could be revealed to him that his prior understanding of what God wanted of him was faulty. Sacrificing a child was not the will of heaven. Within the culture of the time this was a momentous breakthrough. It still is.

In the comments that follow I seek to make transparent the epochal significance of this text. Its subtlety is already hinted at in the opening command to sacrifice Isaac. This summons is less straightforward than it might appear at first sight. To implement the blood sacrifice of his son, Abraham was asked to make a journey to a distant, unspecified location (to "one of the mountains of which I shall tell you"). This meant he would have to travel. Time would elapse, time for certain things to occur.

This sets the stage for the narrative to unfold in progressive stages: first, the preparations for the journey; then the journey itself, culminating on the third day at the base of the mount where the sacrifice was to be made; then the climactic final events associated with the attempted human sacrifice.

1. Preparations

In preparing for the journey Abraham is portrayed as rising early in the morning and setting promptly to work. He does not appear to want to waste a moment implementing the dreadful command that has come to him. Firewood is chopped, an ass is saddled, Isaac and two servants are summoned and the trek to the place of the sacrifice is begun. No words are spoken, no explanations given. The mother, Sarah, is strangely absent—not a hint that she even knew of the dreadful deed that Abraham was now contemplating. A sullen, intense silence hovers over this opening scene.

The British psychiatrist Erich Wellisch, in a sensitive psychological study of this episode,[2] characterizes Abraham during this phase of his ordeal as in a state of moral masochism, as when a father punishes a child. In clinical practice, he writes, fathers are observed who though ostensibly loving toward their sons turn against them with a vengeance. This change, although possibly in preparation for a long time, may occur suddenly, together with an urge for action that seems to be energized by a fanatical sense of necessity to do what is right.

> The moral quality of this power may become particularly obvious if the son's behaviour arouses the father's demand for punishment, as in the case of a teacher whose son falls short in his scholastic achievements, or of a preacher who discovers that his son has misbehaved sexually.
>
> The father may then turn against his son with a severity which is out of proportion to his son's actual

misbehaviour. He attacks him in righteous indignation and with the conviction that he is directed to do so by the highest moral law. But closer observation may reveal that he does so with a heavy heart and that he is at least as much, if not more, distressed about his own attitude against his son as about his son's failure. . . . But at the same time he is bewildered about the apparently moral call in him which orders him to be severe with his son. He is in a state of moral masochism.[3]

It is on this note that the testing of Abraham opens, Wellisch suggests.

2. The Third Day

This awful silence between father and son persists until the third day of their journey, when the second act of this drama opens. Then it was, as they approached the place appointed by God for the sacrifice, that Abraham lifted up his eyes and saw it from afar, as in a vision. This third day experience was regarded in Jewish tradition as being of such tremendous importance that it was thought to have occurred on the first day of the month of Tischri, on Rosh-Hashana, the New Year's Day, when God will judge everything. In another tradition the third day of Abraham's journey coincided with Yom-Kuppur, the Day of Atonement.

At last Abraham speaks, first to his servants, then to his son, and for the first time we are privy to what is going on inside of him, in his heart.

To the servants he says that they should remain with the ass while he and "the lad" (he calls him) go yonder to worship and return again (22:5). Even now he does not tell his son what he is really intent upon doing. Nor is there any reference here to a divine command. Is this a hint that something inside of him is changing—that his moral masochism is weakening, that he is beginning to doubt the righteousness of what he is contemplating doing?

Then we are told how Abraham, still silent, took the wood for the burnt offering and loaded it on his son, while keeping the fire and the knife. With that the two of them went, it is reported (in a phrase repeated at the close of this scene), "both of them together" (22:6, 8).

Now at last father and son speak to each other. It is the son who takes the initiative ("And Isaac said to his father Abraham . . ."). To do so he also had a "testing" to surmount, for he too had been silent to this point, perhaps out of fear or dread of what he imagined his father was about to do. Father and son, Wellisch writes of this and the following scene, were in process of saving *each other*.[4]

"My Father!"

"Here I am, my son,"Abraham replied.

For the first time Abraham speaks *to* his son and calls him "my son." It is an emotional moment.

"Behold the fire and the wood," Isaac asks (he does not mention the knife), "but where is the lamb for a burnt offering?" Isaac still has no inkling, apparently, of the dark thoughts that have been occupying his father during the three days they have been on the road together.

"God will provide himself the lamb for a burnt offering, my son," Abraham replies. This is now the second time he uses these magic words, "my son."

"So they went both of them together" (22:8).

3. Final Events

Scene three takes place on the mountain appointed for the sacrifice (22:9–18). An altar is built and the wood arranged. Abraham binds his son and puts him on the altar on top of the wood. The sentences come swiftly. We marvel that Isaac utters no words of protest, nor resists his father in any way.

It is this moment especially that has gripped the imagination of generations of readers and prompted the caption, "The Binding of Isaac." Abraham's power over his son is now absolute. The son's submission is equally absolute. All is now ready for the father to kill his son. The altar, the wood, the son, the knife, the fire, and, above all, the divine mandate—all are in place.

"Abraham had the right and the power to use the sword,"

Wellisch summarizes, "but he did not use it."[5] Why? Only because a revelation from on high broke through to his consciousness: "*Do not lay your hand on the lad or do anything to him*; for now I know that you fear God, seeing you have not withheld your son, your only son, from me."

At that moment, we are told, Abraham saw a lamb providentially caught in a thicket behind him and offered it instead. Then he called the name of that place: "The Lord [Yahweh] will provide."

The epochal significance of this story is epitomized by Wellisch in the following words:

> As the first of the great patriarchs of the Bible Abraham initiated a new era in the patriarchal order of the world. . . . Love was the principle of the matriarchal order which ruled the world before the patriarchal principle of authority came into being. Abraham, by uniting authority with love, became the creator of the history of Israel.[6]

CONCLUDING COMMENTS

The story recorded in Genesis 22 marks a turning point in the history of the father-involved family. Here at last is a father fully conscious that "heaven" does not want his children abused in a manner to which the cultures of antiquity had become accustomed. Through this story, for the first time in history so far as we know, the absolute power of fathers over their offspring was challenged and they were admonished in no uncertain terms not to harm their children—not to sacrifice them on the altar of their moral masochism. As such Genesis 22 may be regarded as a charter of children's rights, a gift from antiquity for every family on earth.

Notes

1. E. A. Speiser, *Genesis*, The Anchor Bible (New York: Double-day, 1964), p. 164.
2. Erich Wellisch, *Isaac and Oedipus: A Study in Biblical Psychology of the Sacrifice of Isaac: The Akedah* (London: Routledge & Kegan Paul, 1953).
3. *Ibid.*, pp. 98f.
4. *Ibid.*, p. 95.
5. *Ibid.*, p. 93.
6. *Ibid.*, p. 67.

INDEX